HOG HEAVEN

A Guide To South Carolina Barbecue

by **Allie Patricia Wall**

and

Ron L. Layne

Illustrated by Diane Wise Lay

The Sandlapper Store, Inc.

Copyright ©1979 by The Sandlapper Store, Inc.
P.O. Box 841, Lexington, South Carolina 29072

FIRST EDITION

All rights reserved. This book may not be reproduced, in whole or in part, in any form (except for reviews for the public press), without written permission from the publisher.

ISBN 87844-022-4
Manufactured in the United States of America

CONTENTS

Foreword.. v
Barbeque Tradition and the Open Pit......................... 1
Cooking Techniques.. 5
Pit-Cooking It Yourself..................................... 11
Using this Book... 14

DIRECTORY OF SOUTH CAROLINA BARBECUE PLACES

CENTRAL REGION

Leesville	Shealy Bar-B-Q Buffet Style	17
Columbia	Little Pigs Bar-B-Que	18
Lexington	Hites Restaurant	19
West Columbia	Maurice's Piggy Park	21
West Columbia	Oak Grove Bar-B-Q House	23
Columbia	Cowan's Ranch Bar-B-Que	24
Columbia	Midland Kitchen	25
Columbia	The Shady Rest Park	26
Columbia	Smith's Bar-B-Que	27
Columbia	The Pit	28
Columbia	Muldrow's Bar-B-Que	29
Columbia	Porky's Bar-B-Q	30
West Columbia	The Bar-B-Query-J.D. Hite & Son	31
Irmo	Okra Patch	32
Columbia	Sam's Bar-B-Q	33
Eastover	Sike's Bar-B-Q	34
Blythewood	Ray Lever's Bar-B-Q Hut	35
Columbia	Ward's Bar-B-Q	36

SOUTHEAST REGION

Holly Hill, near	Sweatman's Bar-B-Que	37
Charleston	Bessinger's Barbeque House (2)	39
Charleston	Bessinger's Bar-B-Q	40
Mt. Pleasant	Piggy Park	41
Walterboro	Keith's Red Barn	42
North Charleston	Keith's Barbecue	43
Johns Island	Rast's Restaurant	44
Beaufort	Keith's Barbecue	45
Estill, near	Lester's Pit Bar-B-Q	46
Hampton	Fennell's Bar-B-Q	47
St. George	Duke's BBQ	48
Summerville	Drozes Bar-B-Q	48
Orangeburg	Duke's BBQ	49
Orangeburg	Duke's Bar-B-Q	50
Orangeburg	Brown Derby Bar-B-Q	51
Cameron	Earl Duke's Bar-B-Q	52
North	Laird's Bar-B-Q	53
Hardeeville	Rogers Bar-B-Que	55

NORTHEAST REGION

Andrews	Moree's Bar-B-Q	57
Kingstree, near	Tisdale's Bar-B-Q	58
Scranton	Country Cousin Bar-B-Que	59
Lake City	Fred Gaskins' Grocery	60
Lake City	Owen's Bar-B-Q	61
Florence	Cain's Bar-B-Q	62
Florence	Woody's Barbecue	63
Florence	Bob's Bar-B-Q	64
Nichols	Daniel's and Ray's Barbecue	65
Aynor	Pinetucket Bar-B-Q Barn	66

Conway	Radd Dew's Bar-B-Q	67
Windy Hill Beach	The Red Barn Bar-B-Q	68
Hemingway, near	Big D's Bar-B-Q I	69
Surfside Beach	Big D's Bar-B-Q II	70

SOUTH CENTRAL REGION

Newberry	The 'Que Pit	71
Newberry	Wise's Bar-B-Q	72
Prosperity	Stockman's Bar-B-Q Place	73
Aiken	Fulmer's Bar-B-Q	74
New Ellenton	Crosby's Bar-B-Q	74
New Ellenton	Carolina Bar-B-Q	75
Beech Island	Chavous Pit Cooked Bar-B-Q	76
Beech Island	Smokey Porkers Bar-B-Q	77
Beech Island	Freeman's BBQ	78
North Augusta	Edmunds Bar-B-Que	79
Aiken	Edmunds Bar-B-Que	80
North Augusta	Barbeque Diner	81
North Augusta	Country Pit Bar-B-Que	82
North Augusta	Lee's Bar-B-Q	83
Barnwell	Black's Bar-B-Q	84
Barnwell	Bo-Corley's Bar-B-Q	85
Bamberg	Mett's Bar-B-Q	86
Denmark	Ed Neeley's Bar-B-Q	87
Fairfax	Dukes BBQ	88

NORTH CENTRAL REGION

Winnsboro	David Brown's House Pit Bar-B-Q	89
Hartsville	Westwood Bar-B-Q	90
Union	Midway BBQ	92
Chester	Buddy's Hickory Cooked Bar-B-Q	93
Fort Mill	Fat Willy's Hawg House	93
Rock Hill	Fat Willy's Hawg House	93
Gaffney	Willard's BBQ and Hash House	94
Great Falls	Hilltop Restaurant	95
Ridgeway	Boney's Bar-B-Que	96
Kershaw	Broome's Restaurant	97
McBee	Little Betsy's Bar-B-Q Rest.	98
Chesterfield	Shiloh BBQ	99
Bennettsville	Revel's Barbecue Center	100
Camden	Reynold's Bar-B-Q	101
Elgin	Hammy's Bar-B-Q House	102
Sumter (4)	Ward's Bar-B-Q	103
Sumter	Bar-B-Q Hut Restaurant	104
Manning	D & H Bar-B-Q	105

NORTHWEST REGION

Spartanburg	Sawgrass Jim's Bar-B-Q House	107
Spartanburg	Beacon Drive-In	109
Spartanburg	Sheridan's Restaurant	110
Anderson	The Ranch House Barbecue	111
Anderson	The Chatter Box	112
Anderson	Little Pigs Barbeque of Anderson	113
Greenwood	Rick's Bar-B-Q	113
Greenwood	Little Pigs of Greenwood	114
Spartanburg	Old Hickory Restaurant	115
Mauldin	Pig-N-Chick	116
Greenville	Little Pigs Barbecue	117
Greenville	Little Pigs Barbecue	118
Index...		119

FOREWORD

Skeptics might say that there are no crazier people than those who would drive 70 miles just to eat good barbecue. They are wrong. Crazier still are those who would travel 5,000 miles (within a single state) to write about where to eat good barbecue. But that is just what we did.

The idea for the book came one day as I was feasting on Sweatman's barbecued pork and ribs in Eutawville. I found myself wondering if Sweatman's was really as great as I thought it was. Just to satisfy my curiosity, I decided to find out by sampling other barbecue throughout the state. One place led to another, and the surprising differences and similarities convinced me that someone needed to write a book about barbecue in South Carolina and provide a directory of places for barbecue enthusiasts like me. After all, some of the best places seemed to be tucked away in remote areas that only the local people knew. Realizing that the task of covering the entire state of South Carolina was impossible to do alone, I convinced a friend to be my co-author.

During the next five months we travelled the Low Country, Piedmont, Foothills, and Netherlands of the state, in search of the epitome of South Carolina barbecue. Our expeditions were truly "trials by fire," as we learned about the traditions, techniques, and monumental efforts involved in the preparation of this renown Southern treat.

One of the most rewarding aspects of our journeys was getting to know the South Carolina barbecuepreneurs. Convincing these wary barbecue specialists that we were not out to steal their sauce recipes or their cooking techniques was our first obstacle. Once persuaded, most of the owners became keenly interested in our project, often supplying more information than was expected. Although we met our share of ill-tempered, suspicious, sometimes hostile proprietors, by far the majority were friendly, helpful, and enthusiastic about educating a couple of novices in the ways of barbecuing.

Along the way we made some interesting discoveries about barbecue cooking in South Carolina:

- On any given Thursday over 80,000 pounds of pork (the equivalent of 8,000 fair sized hogs) hit pits, grills, ovens, and cookers around the state.
- Enough hash is set to simmering to fill a small farm pond.
- A small forest is consumed to provide enough wood for the open pit-cooking of pork, beef, and ribs.
- Pride in their barbecue is often more important than profit to many of these people of the pits.

To write this book we ate at least five ounces of barbecue-related food at each place - a grand total of 30 pounds. Our cars consumed even more than our stomachs. If computed at 20¢ per mile (the standard rate for gasoline consumption and wear and tear on the car), the barbecue-pursuing journeys cost us over $1,000.

Was it worth it? If it saves you one mile or one wrong turn in your efforts to find a truly memorable barbecue, then we believe it was. Naturally, there are bound to be a few places we have overlooked. But, this book represents the most comprehensive guide of its kind.

And how do I feel about Sweatman's after 5,000 miles and over 100 barbecue tastings? It's still the best in my book, though it has some strong contenders nipping at its pits.

August 1979   Allie Patricia Wall

BARBECUE TRADITION AND THE OPEN PIT

BARBECUE. If the derivation of the word "barbecue" is the source of heated debate among open pit enthusiasts of the world, it is only in keeping pace with the deviation of spelling in the word itself. It seems there are at least ten different ways to spell what you produce when you pit-cook meat (usually pork) over the glowing hot coals and succulent smoke of burned hickory, oak, or hardwood. The number of different spellings is nearly matched by the number of stories people tell about how barbecue got its name.

While no barbecue aficionado attempts to date barbecue back to The Creation, some of the tales date pretty far back into the past, and more than one of those stories is a little far-fetched.

One of the more etymologically based claims concerning the name suggests that the word is a derivative of an Aztec Indian root word. The story goes that Cortez and his merry band of pillagers were skirting the area around Acapulco when they saw Indians drying fish on makeshift racks made of interwoven branches. The Indians supplied Cortez with a name for the racks and/or technique, the Spaniard bastardized the word a little, and it cropped up as "barbacoa" in the Spanish language.

Another story of etymological design reveals that "barbecue" was borrowed from the French term "barbe-a-queue." The word, meaning "beard-to-tail," was in reference to the fact that whole animals are cooked - hoof to head.

One of the more outlandish stories (though widely accepted) concerning the naming of pit-cooked meat gives the United States credit for christening barbecue. (See July, 1979, Sandlapper, "The Quest for the Best Barbecue in the World" by Orin Anderson). The story goes that an Englishman named Bernard Quayle (you're beginning to get the idea) moved to this country at about the time the New World was realizing its potential. A Hugh Hefner-like party thrower, Bernard would prepare feasts for friends and family by roasting assorted game and livestock over mammoth open pits. Bernard Quayle's gala gourmet affairs were the social events of the day. They were so popular, in fact, that (and I quote) "...the name of his ranch became a byword for pit-cooking and outdoor feasting: the-BQ." And so it goes...

At least one part of the Bernard Quayle tale has a ring of truth. In the plantation-South, events such as the Quayle feasts were both frequent and prodigious. The word barbecue, already established as meaning the product and the cooking process, took on a third meaning. Barbecue came to mean the event itself. Hickory smoke carried by the wind over the low-country around Charleston was the invitation to a delightful party. Barbecues became the social events - bar none.

It became commonplace in those days to see men slaving (literally) over hollowed portions of earth, continually feeding the pits with a fresh supply of glowing hickory or oak coals brought from a blazing fire at no short distance from the pit. Makeshift racks were often used for holding whole hogs above the coals, or the pork was impaled on a shaft that would support its weight while the smoke and heat of the pit transformed it from a mere slaughtered hog to a succulent feast for family and friends of the plantation owner. The smoke and smell of the wood-fed pit would usually mean a gathering of kin and a cause for celebration. The activity of the soot-faced men tending the pit (guarding against pit fires and overdone meat) was matched in the final hours of cooking by the frenzy of preparation in the plantation kitchen where the other traditional barbecue dishes were being readied for the feast.

For our great-grandfathers (mere children then), the blazing fire and the hissing of the pit made for brightly-lit imaginations and provided wood-burned memories of a tradition they would carry forward with them into manhood. Years later, they would remember those sooty sentries of the pits whose efforts had brought such tasty rewards. Full grown, they looked for men who could practice the culinary discipline required of the barbecue expert and would teach their children to respect the talent of those barbecue impresarios. The pit barbecue became one of the few holdovers from the antebellum South, sparking memories of the grandeur lost in the turning of the century.

Memories are not erased easily, but they do fade with each successive generation. Time produces children who no longer associate glowing coals with barbecued pork. In a century marked by a constant pursuit of convenience, toil gives way to technology. The open pits are being filled; becoming the subject of stories rather than the site of pig-roasting rituals.

But ease of cooking isn't the only reason the barbecue men of our time are switching in ever-increasing numbers to such convenient cooking methods as electric pits, gas ovens, and charcoal cookers. Many of them are being pushed from their pits by laws that place sanitation far above the sanctity of traditional barbecuing.

It is stated in the South Carolina regulations governing Bar-B-Q establishments (Form FSB 71-1) that "...rotary equipment and cooking cabinets are strongly recommended for ease of cleaning and simplicity of operation." To reinforce this idea, today's legislation has driven the pits indoors; requiring a four sided, ceilinged shelter for the open pits. The result is that now the hottest of culinary art forms gets even hotter. Where once a cool breeze cut some of the heat away from the pits, today the pit area becomes a veritable oven. Concrete floors are now required around the pit and sand must be placed in layers on the bottom of the pit and replaced periodically. If cleaning a pit was work in the open air, imagine the work required of men shoveling greasy sand from the pits only to be faced with the prospect of then weaving their way out-of-doors with the mess. Barbecue pit owners face a monstrous task.

While bona fide, licensed barbecue establishment owners are pushed indoors (raising overhead and angry complaints), the so-called "occasional barbecue cookers" seem to enjoy free reign in the preparation of their pork. You know the situation: A volunteer fire-department or local civic organization needs to raise some money, so they dig a hole, buy some hogs, and, BINGO - they're in business. Legislation is ignored and barbecue establishment owners shake their heads in utter disbelief at the inequity of the situation. Considering the frequency with which some groups have such fund raisers, it is no small wonder the barbecue people are outraged. Caged in their sheltered pits, they must throw up their hands in disgust and watch their profit margin dwindle. Granted, the legislation is meant to protect the consumer and the environment. Open pits are notorious fly traps, pollution producers, and danger zones, but moving the pits indoors may be producing something equally dangerous...

Open pits (and sheltered open pits) require fairly constant attention. Pit fires are commonplace due to the grease rolling from the cooking pork onto the glowing embers at the base of the pit. With an unsheltered open pit, the risk of injury was bad enough. With a ceilinged shelter, the potential for a real disaster is ever present. So the legislators push the barbecue owners indoors and the threat of a costly fire (life and/or property) pushes an ever-increasing number of them toward an electric cooker.

COOKING TECHNIQUES

With the decline of the open pit came some new-fangled methods of cooking barbecue. Restaurant owners discovered the advantages of modern technology: faster cooking, easier cooking, less labor, cleaner food and facilities, less danger of fires. One method used in about 40% of the barbecue places visited in South Carolina is the electric cooker.

By far the majority of electric cookers used in these barbecue establishments are manufactured by Bar-B-Q King (a company in Greenville) or Bar-B-Q Slave. Both companies, and there are many others, manufacture similar products. Generally, the electric cooker is made of stainless steel or some other heavy-duty metal and has a lid (with dampers) that remains closed during cooking. The meat is placed on a metal rack inside the cooker, the temperature set, the lid closed, and the owner can walk away, leaving it completely unattended. Electric heating elements, located in the lid and on either side near the bottom of the cooker, are similar to those in an ordinary electric oven. Metal shields protect the elements from any dripping grease. On the sloping bottom is an opening that allows the grease to drain, and a pan underneath catches the drippings.

Almost all electric cookers come equipped with a smoke box or a metal plate that will hold chips of hickory, oak, or other hard wood. Soft wood (pine and spruce, for example) is generally too sappy and emits a resinous, sooty smoke. While the meat is cooking, the wood can be burned (or on the plate it is ignited by the hot electrical element touching it), thus producing smoke that penetrates the meat and gives it that hearty wood-smoke flavor barbecue connoisseurs crave.

Electric cookers come in all sizes -- from small ones that hold six 12-pound shoulders to large ones that can accommodate four whole hogs.

Varying as much as or more than the electric cookers in size and construction are gas cookers. Like the electric ones, some are constructed of heavy metal. But many of the gas cookers in South Carolina barbecue establishments are long four-sided concrete block pits with gas lines running on both sides, lengthwise. Above these gas lines shallow metal trays (approximately eight inches wide) containing water disperse heat and shield the lines from dripping grease that could start uncontrollable fires. The convenience of this cooking apparatus is that with one match and a

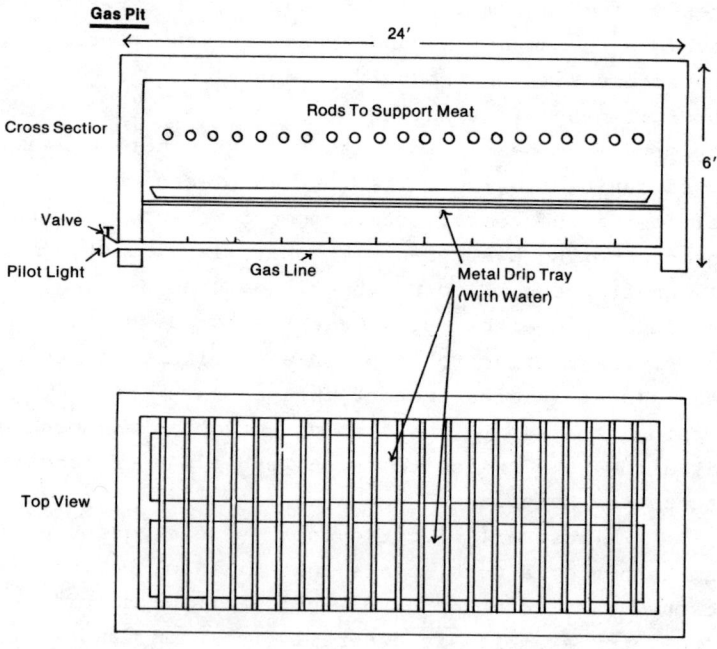

flip of the hand, the pilot can be lighted and the gas fire can be turned down low to cook the meat very slowly or turned up high to cook fast. The meat, which is covered either by a metal lid or by large sheets of corrugated paper to keep in the heat and smoke, cannot be left completely unattended, though, since it cooks only on one side at a time. Some barbecue chefs believe in turning the meat several times during eight hours of cooking. Others believe that, after cooking fat-side-up for about six hours, it should then be turned to cook on the other side for about two more hours. To turn or not to turn: That is the question that will probably still be debated in the centuries to come.

Another cooking technique that is used by a smattering of barbecue places across the state is charcoal cooking. One enterprising barbecuer, Henry Rast of John's Island, after fifteen years of experimentation with charcoal, has developed and patented his own barbecuing technique: the stainless steel PDG (Pretty Darn Quick) Cooker. In an article published in the March 1978 issue of <u>Outdoor</u> <u>Life</u>, Mr. Rast explained, "My cooking secret was a new concept in cookers -- a covered barbecue pit. It applies heat indirectly, and evenly, to seal in natural flavor. The narrow fireboxes are located on opposite sides (rather than underneath), and the meat cooks on a grill directly over a drip pan, so there are no fire flareups from fat and no dense clouds of smoke inside. This cooks meat while retaining the juices."

But many barbecue places in South Carolina that cook with charcoal do not require such fancy technology. Smith's Barbecue in Columbia is the perfect example of an operation that has changed very little during the past eighteen years and has not yet succumbed to the implementation of modern equipment. In one corner of Smith's is an old brick fireplace. Manager Sam West starts the charcoal there, and after it has burned down to a white glow, he transfers the coals to the bottom of long concrete pit nearby. Little by little, the pit is heated with the burning coals, and the meat is then placed on sturdy metal racks about a foot and a half above the coal bed. Corrugated paper covers the meat, keeping the heat and flavor inside and keeping the flies outside. Smith's even has a small charcoal-heated pit that keeps the meat warm until it is ready to be served.

Only a bit more sophisticated are the closed brick ovens, some of which use coke or hardwood lump charcoal (various kinds of hardwood -- oak, hickory, ash, maple, for instance) compressed into briquets. Still other such closed pits use oak and hickory. The advantage of the closed pit is that it cooks more efficiently and evenly, allowing the smoke produced by hot grease and fat dripping on the coals to penetrate the meat. The Ranch House Barbecue in Anderson burns

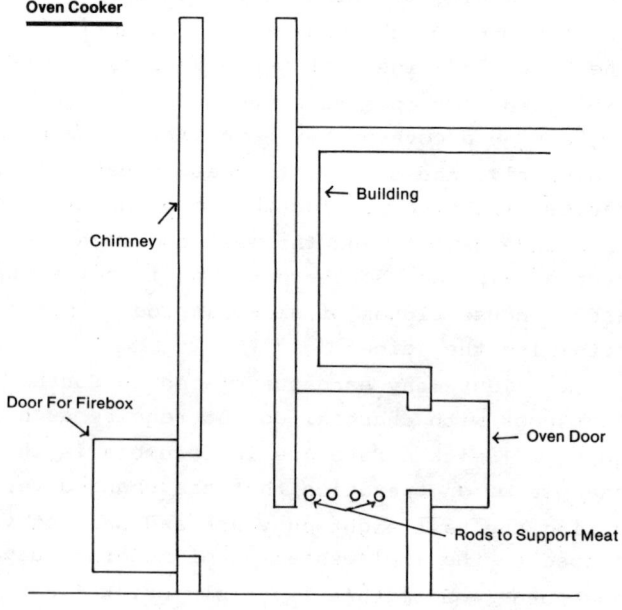

hickory and red oak in their closed brick oven. An opening in the back of the chimney allows easy access for stoking the fire and removing the ashes, and little heat or smoke is lost in the process. A natural draft draws the smoke up the chimney by way of a large oven where the meat is placed on sturdy metal grills.

Similar to this method is the one used at Sawgrass Jim's in Spartanburg, at Cowan's in Columbia and at David Brown's in Winnsboro. The technique is different from the one just described only in that the compartment where the fire is built is separate. Vents permit heat and smoke to be sucked through to an oven where the meat is cooked, or cured. No flareups can occur because the fire is not directly under the meat.

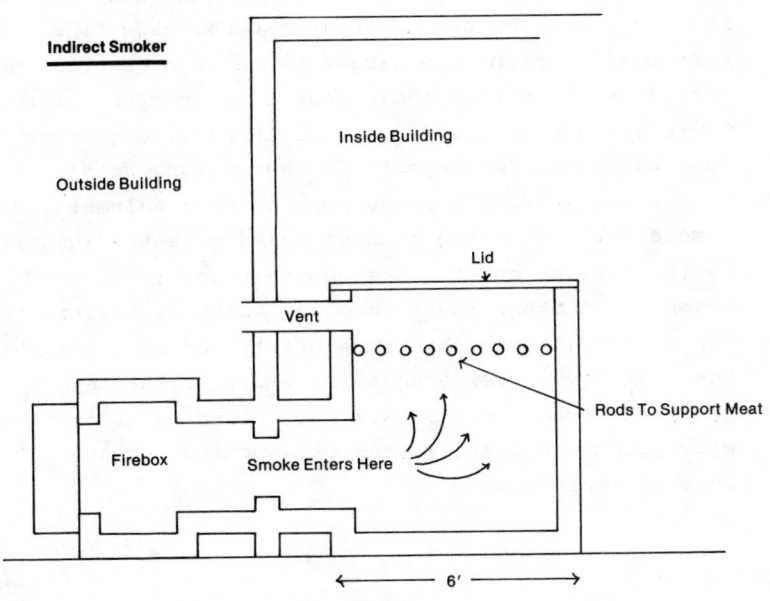

Of all these methods, electric cooking seems to be the direction barbecue cooking is heading. Robert Laird, for instance, of Laird's Bar-B-Q in North, South Carolina, served his barbecue apprenticeship near an open pit, then developed a sophisticated gas pit for his own operation, but he is looking toward the day when electric pits will serve his purpose. His claim that technique and sauce, not heat source, make the difference in taste is shared by an ever-increasing number of barbecue chefs.

Barbecue sauces in South Carolina vary as much as cooking techniques, but they usually fall into four general categories: mustard-based (usually tangy or tart), tomato-based (usually sweet and mild), vinegar-based (usually spicy-peppery), and mustard/ketchup-based (with broad variations in flavor). Again, these are generalizations wide open for debate by all barbecue lovers -- connoisseurs and lay persons.

A number of barbecue establishments have built their reputations around their sauces, as well as their barbecue. Some of the larger barbecue operations have facilities to bottle their sauces for commercial sales. These include Ray Lever's in Blythewood, Oak Grove in West Columbia, Bessinger's in Charleston, Ward's in Sumter and Maurice's Piggy Park in West Columbia, to name a few. Over-the-counter sales of sauce (usually by the pint or quart) is a common practice in the majority of other South Carolina barbecue businesses.

While many barbecue practitioners profess that the technique, fuel source, or sauce is the key to great barbecue, only an artistic blending of the three will produce a feast worthy of sporting Bernard Quayle's initials.

PIT-COOKING IT YOURSELF

You'll never appreciate the work that goes into producing real barbecue until you've pit-cooked it yourself. The following guide gives a step-by-step approach for preparing barbecue the open pit way.

MATERIALS NEEDED:

Shovel

40-50 fireplace-size logs (oak or hickory)

4-1/2' x 4-1/2' piece of heavy gauge wire mesh

8-10 15-pound cement blocks (total weight of blocks should exceed weight of pig)

One whole hog (100 pounds or less) split lengthwise

Water or sand for extinguishing fires

Paint brush (new)

One gallon of sauce (Most cookbooks offer various sauces recipes. A vinegar/pepper combination is one of the best basting mixtures).

In a cleared, open area dig a 2 feet deep hole, 3-1/2 feet in diameter. Cover the hole with heavy gauge wire mesh, securing three sides with cement blocks and leaving an opening at one side of the pit for adding fresh coals (see illustration). In a clear area about 15 feet from the pit build a fire. One built with 10 logs should provide sufficient coal base for the pit. Allow the fire to burn until the coals are white. Using the shovel, transfer hot coals to the pit. Spread an even layer under the wire. Maintain the hickory fire in the open area so that hot coals can be constantly added to the pit.

Place hog fat-side-up on the wire. After several hours, thoroughly baste the pig with sauce, using the paint brush. Continue intermittent basting every hour. After 10 hours, turn the hog so that the fat side is down. This will ensure thorough cooking. While small flames (caused by dripping grease) are normal, a blazing fire will ruin the meat.

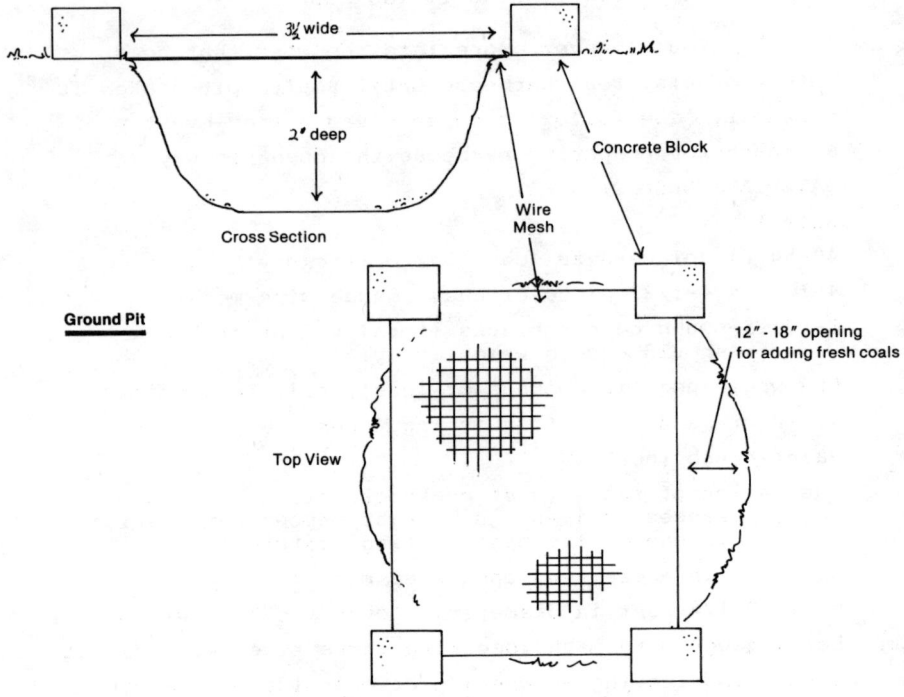

At the end of 12 hours remove the hog and extinguish the fire and coals in the pit. The pork should contain a little fat, but excess amounts should be trimmed. Rib portions should be cut from the hog and select pork should be stripped from the bones. Pork can be chopped or sliced and served with or without additional sauce.

An alternative to a ground pit is a cement block structure that can be easily constructed. The structure will require approximately 35 cement blocks, fashioned in the manner shown in illustration.

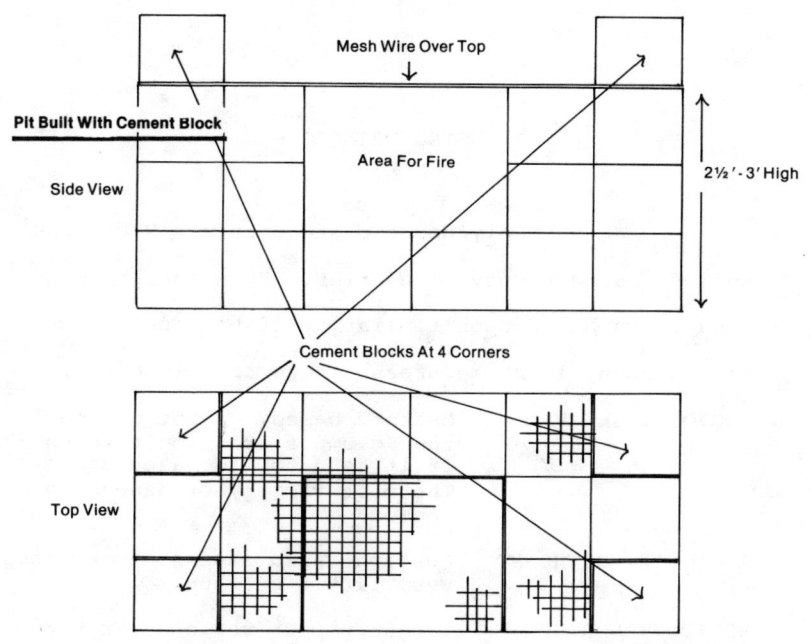

PORK ANATOMY

While it does not take a butcher to figure out where to find the ribs on a hog, some cuts of pork may be hard to distinguish if you are a novice barbequer. A prime example of this is found with the very mention of the words "Boston butts." The butt is that lean portion of pork found almost as far from the tail as a butcher can chop. The place on the pork torso where the shoulders and the front legs "butt" up against it is the home of the Boston butts. Bar-B-Q houses that offer customers this cut of meat have insured that they will lose less serving meat after cooking due to the lean meat portions.

Pork shoulders are located at the upper extreme of the front legs where the butts blend with the leg, and pork hams are found in the same region at the top of the back legs.

Seekers of pork loins will find these cuts running down the side of the hog between the Boston butts and the hams. Just below the loin, near the under side or stomach of the hog, you will find the bacon; a cut of meat that quickly disappears when the pig is placed on the hot coals of a glowing pit.

USING THIS BOOK

We have divided the state into six distinct regions using county boundaries. Even though regions were drawn based upon similarity of barbecue types and sauces found in these areas, there is some overlapping

REGION 1 CENTRAL — Mustard-based. A lot of people in the Columbia area won't touch it if it is a tomato-based sauce. The most variety of sauces in any region.

REGION 2 SOUTHEAST — Mustard-based sauces, some vinegar, very little ketchup.

REGION 3 NORTHEAST — Vingar/pepper region. This region is also the home of chicken bog.

REGION 4 SOUTH CENTRAL — The sauces run about 50-50 on the mustard and ketchup-based.

REGION 5 NORTH CENTRAL — The closer to the central part of this region the more mustard used. This is the conglomerate district. Includes mixtures of ketchup and mustard.

REGION 6 NORTHWEST — Tomato region (red clay country) Even in this region, the closer to Columbia you travel, there is a marked increase in the use of mustard sauce. Chili/sweet relish sauce surfaces in and around Spartanburg, but it, too, makes use of ketchup ingredient.

THE ESTABLISHMENT INVENTORY

1) LOCATION: We have given the address, geographic location, and telephone number of each establishment. In our travels across

the state we have found that the best source for directions to these barbecue houses is service station attendants.

2) HOURS: While you can generally rely on the hours listed in the directory, if planning to travel a long distance to visit these places, you should phone ahead. Vacations, holidays and seasonal changes will often result in a fluctuation of business hours. Phoning ahead is also advisable because the mortality rate of unestablished barbecue restaurants is high.

3) TYPE: "Type" refers to the kind of restaurant and the services provided, i.e. regular menu, buffet, take-out, drive-through, curb service and catering.

4) PRICES: Barbecue prices in South Carolina do not vary tremendously. In fact we have noted only a few places where prices were excessively high or low. In reviewing prices (May-June, 1979) we have developed the following scales:

	TAKE-OUT (bulk meat prices)	EAT-IN (buffet)	(dinner)
Low	Under $3.25	Under $3.50	Under $2.75
Average	$3.25-$4.25	$3.50-$4.25	$2.75-$3.50
High	Over $4.25	Over $4.25	Over $3.50

5) TECHNIQUE: Guide entries note the method employed by each restaurant. For a detailed discussion of particular barbecue techniques, refer to the section on "Cooking Techniques".

6) THE BARBECUE: Included in this section are brief histories of the establishments, comments on methods of barbecue preparation, descriptions of barbecue and sauces, and notes on menu specialty items.

7) THE PLACE: We have described the facilities, physical surroundings, and atmosphere of every place - from the ramshackled hominess of Midway Bar-B-Q, to the spit-shined starkness of Ray Lever's. Our experience has been that you cannot gauge the quality of the food by the quality of the building. Some of the most delectable barbecue in South Carolina can be found in the seediest surroundings.

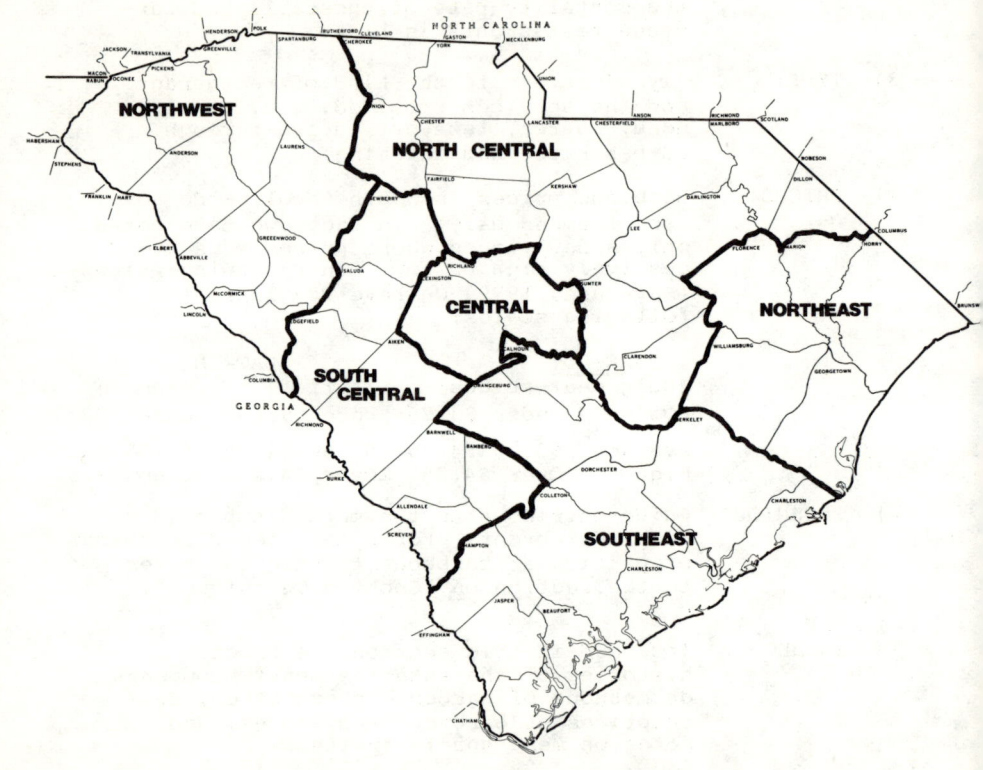

****

CENTRAL REGION

****

SHEALY BAR-B-Q BUFFET STYLE

LOCATION: One block from Leesville's main business district on Hwy. 1 in Leesville 523-5481

HOURS: Mon.-Tues. and Thurs.-Sat. 11:30 a.m. - 9 p.m.

TYPE: Buffet, take-out and catering

PRICES: Buffet-low to average; Bulk rates-average.

COOKING TECHNIQUE: Combination gas/charcoal pit

THE BARBECUE:

A visit to Shealy Bar-B-Q is a lesson in hard work. The Shealy operation is as fast-paced as that of Bessinger's in Charleston. Everywhere you turn you will see someone involved in the preparation or serving of fine pork barbecue. After one decade of business, Victor and Sarah Shealy own an extremely popular barbecue house, one that has survived a disastrous pit fire to become a booming success. Victor, a former night watchman, and Sarah, a former grocery clerk, turned a florist's building into one of the most populated pork houses in the South. It is not uncommon on Friday evenings to see a long line of folks waiting outside the pastel green building for their chance at the Shealys' renown buffet. After numerous additions to the building, Shealy's is being remodeled this year to make room for a growing clientele.

Cooked on a gas/charcoal pit, Shealy's pork is sauced with a mustard-based mixture as soon as it leaves the grill. Fourteen hours of even cooking and the mustard-based sauce produced a moist, lean barbecue. The addition of extra sauce resulted in mouthwatering barbecue that was well worth a long drive and short wait. And if the barbecue isn't enough, Sarah Shealy works on the other angles of human appetites. The buffet includes fried chicken, fresh vegetables, vegetable soup, milk gravy, slaw, potato salad, pickles, rolls, corn muffins, biscuits (lunch time only) and a salad bar stocked with no fewer than 18 items. The Shealys believe in feeding folks right, and their high volume business allows them to give their customers one of the most generous buffet menus anywhere. "We make a good living," Sarah Shealy will tell you. "We have a good volume business, and most people can't understand how we sell it (the barbecue) as cheap as we do." Despite the financial security the business allows the Shealy family, Sarah works every day from 6 a.m. until closing. She loves her customers and her business, though she is quick to admit, "I sure didn't dream it would get this big!"

THE PLACE:

The pit area and front dining rooms at Shealy's are the original landmarks of an operation that has enjoyed constant growth. The soft green color of the Shealy barbecue house has since been spread over numerous building additions. Today, three dining rooms filled with folding chairs and tables provide seating for up to 250 customers. Business has always been bigger than building space at Shealy's, and that is still true today. A take-out and a bulk meat sales counter is provided for the transient members of the Shealy clientele.

* * * * * * *

LITTLE PIGS BAR-B-QUE

LOCATION: 4927 Alpine Rd. (Located between the Blue Cross/Blue Shield Building and Alpine Baptist Church), Columbia 788-8238

HOURS: Thurs.-Sat. 11 a.m. - 9 p.m.

TYPE: Buffet, take-out and catering.

PRICES: Buffet - average; Bulk rates - average

COOKING
TECHNIQUE: Electric cooker - hickory-smoked

THE BARBECUE:

In 1963 Lawrence Britton opened the Little Pigs Bar-B-Q (then affiliated with the Little Pigs of America chain) in the Rosewood Shopping Center in Columbia, where he served barbecue for many years. In June 1978 he opened this establishment on the other side of town, and many of his old customers have followed him over. To prepare the chopped barbecue, Mr. Britton cooks pork shoulders for about 15 hours on an electric cooker that contains a hickory-smoking apparatus. After the meat is stripped from the bone and chopped, he soaks it in his special tomato-based sauce. According to Britton, his barbecue tastes best if it has been soaked in the sauce for two or three days. The sauce, a tomato-based mixture sweetened with sugar, is popular enough to warrant selling by the pint. The chopped barbecue (the string variety) was moist and had a sweet hickory flavor. The ribs and chicken, also hickory-smoked throughout the cooking process, are thoroughly sauced after they have cooked. The result is quite palate-pleasing! The meaty ribs were drenched in their tangy sauce, and the chicken was so tender it fell apart when touched. Another speciality of which Lawrence Britton is quite proud is the hash, made of 1/3 pork and 2/3 beef. To complete the buffet (all-you-can-eat), pork skins (cooked, then deep fat fried for 15 minutes) and rinds, yams, slaw, green beans, peaches, smoked barbecue beans, pickles and rolls are made available. Britton reports that his barbecue business suffers from no slack period. The summer is an excellent catering time (over one ton of barbeque is sold just on the 4th of July), as are Thanksgiving and Christmas seasons.

THE PLACE:

The dining area of the Little Pigs is one large room containing metal folding tables and chairs (seating 125). The self-service buffet is kept well-stocked by the conscientious employees. Extra tea, barbecue sauce, and condiments are set up within easy reach of the customers.

* * * * * * *

HITES RESTAURANT

LOCATION: Intersection of Hwy. 1 and 378, Lexington 359-2589

HOURS: Mon.-Sat. 6 a.m. - 10 p.m.

PRICES: Dinners-average; take out-average

TYPE: Regular menu, take-out and catering

COOKING
TECHNIQUE: Electric cooker - hickory-smoked

THE BARBECUE:

In 1947 when Harry and Betty Ann Hite opened their restaurant, they called it "Ten-to-One" because

-19-

of its hours of operation. It has the distinction of being Lexington's oldest eating establishment. Back then the Hites barbecued whole hogs on a hole-in-the-ground pit. When the restaurant was torn down in 1953, a cement block building was erected to replace it. With the boom in the barbecue business the Hites were forced to modernize their cooking technique to make their operation more efficient and productive. So, about 1957, they filled the pit and purchased electric cookers with hickory smokers.

   Today the Hites pride themselves on their barbecue's high reputation. In fact, Betty Ann Hite said several times, "If we give out of barbecue we'll close the restaurant" - even though the Hites' menu includes much more than barbecue. Shoulders and hams are cooked for 8 hours on electric cookers and smoked with hickory. After the meat has been chopped (Mr. Hite prefers to chop his pork into extra large chunks), it is mixed with a mustard-based sauce that has a long history. The large chunks of barbecue, containing not the slightest trace of fat, were moist and had a pleasant hickory flavor. The pieces cut from the exterior portions of the meat were crisp and chewy; they possessed a great hickory taste. A little spicy, the beef hash was hearty, not runny. Sold by the pint, the quart or the gallon, the mild mustard sauce was a pleasant accompaniment to the barbecue - without overshadowing the hickory taste of the meat. Customers are served generous portions of the Hites' barbecue in sandwiches and on plates with hash and rice, french fries, and a salad from the salad bar. Occasionally, a barbecue buffet is offered, but generally the customer orders from the menu, which includes a wide variety of non-barbecue entrees such as country ham, quail, lobster, steaks and seafood.

THE PLACE:

   One part of Hites Restaurant is the Dairy Bar, a small building that is separated from the main one. The main building is composed of light yellow cement blocks and a wood-shingled roof. In one long room is a counter with about 10 stools. The room is lined with large picture windows covered with mini-blinds. For short orders and quick service, this is the place to eat. For those who desire more comfortable surroundings there are five separate dining rooms. All are carpeted, wall-papered, and similar in their funishings. The largest of the rooms is the Colony Room, partly wood-paneled and partly wall-papered. A patterned carpet and homey lighting fixtures make the room more comfortable. Wooden tables for four or more are covered with yellow cloths and have wooden "captain" chairs. Total seating capacity is 235.

* * * * * * *

MAURICE'S PIGGY PARK

LOCATION: Knox Abbott Extension and Airport Rd., West Columbia 796-0220

HOURS: Mon.-Sat. 10 a.m. - 11 p.m.

TYPE: Regular menu, take out and curb service

PRICES: Dinners-average; Bulk rates-average.

COOKING TECHNIQUE: Closed pit - hickory

THE BARBECUE:

Maurice Bessinger and his brother, Melvin, opened their first Piggy Park in Charleston in 1953. In six months the converted Zesto was doing the biggest volume sales of all drive-ins in South Carolina. Shortly afterward, the brothers' partnership was dissolved, and Maurice moved to West Columbia, where he opened the present Piggy Park. At one time Bessinger operated as many as eight barbecue establishments in four cities. Now he has just one and is content running it. He refuses to franchise, even though requests to do so are frequent, and he has even stopped promoting catering. The barbecue technique has changed very little over the past 25 years. About eighteen years ago Bessinger experimented with some modern barbecue-cooking machinery, but he refused to compromise. He insists that no matter how sophisticated the technology, nothing can equal the taste of fresh pork cooked over hickory.

During an average year about 5,000 hogs are cooked to make Bessinger's renown barbecue. On a large closed pit that can accommodate 100 hams at a time, Bessinger cooks the pork about 18 hours, seasoning the meat a little during the process. Maurice's sells its barbecue by the plate, basket, sandwich, or pound: barbecued pork, beef, pork ribs, chicken and hash. Three sauces, which Mr. Bessinger bottles at a nearby plant and sells commercially, are the Regular (containing mustard, apple cider vinegar, soy sauce, peppers, and other spices); the Hickory (similar except with hickory flavoring); and the Spicy Hot (with an extra dash of hot peppers and spices). The most popular is the regular. Slightly sweet with a zippy taste, it makes an excellent addition to the chopped pork.

The barbecued pork was cut into large chunks (some of the biggest we've found) of moist, rich meat. The crustier, well-cooked outside pieces had a delicious taste of hickory. The lean barbecue was served with a little sauce poured over it, and the customer may add more if he desires. The pork ribs were some of the meatiest ones we have tasted. They had a rich, slightly sweet flavor and a spicy taste that put a tingle in the mouth. A light, hickory-smoked flavor emerged from the chewy, well-cooked exterior. Like the chopped barbecue, the juicy ribs were accompanied by the tangy, mustard-based sauce. These were definitely "5-napkin" ribs! To make his hash, Bessinger uses only fresh hog jowls and livers. Other menu items include pork skins, hamburgers, fried chicken, shrimp, hush puppies, onion rings, and desserts such as "Antebellum chocolate cake."

THE PLACE:

One of the most impressive parts of the barbecue establishment is the curb-service operation. The tin-covered drive-in slots (complete with lighted menu, speaker, and trash bag) number 62. Waitresses wearing navy blue pleated skirts, white blouses, and red bandanas deliver the orders quickly, true to the "3 Minute Service" motto. Bessinger noted that his is one of the largest curb-service operations in the U.S. A tall stack of hickory beside a soot-blackened chimney is almost as eye-catching as the giant American flag that flies over the operation. Written in bold white letters on the roof of the restaurant is "Old South Barbecue." Maurice's is not easy to miss.

Inside the brick restaurant building are two small dining rooms that seat a total of 85 people. One dining room is designed to look old-fashioned and country-ish. In it are ordinary wooden tables and ladder-back chairs, a black wood-burning stove, wagon wheels, and various antiques. Several large round tables are topped with lazy-susans. Crisp calico curtains and hanging plants adorn the windows. At the entrance to the dining area is a walk-up order counter. After the customer has placed his order and taken a seat, a waitress serves the food. The other dining room has fewer frills. Booths with six individual fold-down seats occupy most of the space. Calico curtains decorate the windows, and photographs of people enjoying barbecue adorn the woodpaneled walls. Wafting throughout the restaurant (and for a block in every direction) is the appetite-teasing aroma of hickory.

* * * * * * *

OAK GROVE BAR-B-Q HOUSE

LOCATION: On Oak Road, off U.S. 1 between Lexington and West Columbia 356-3434

HOURS: Fri. and Sat. 11 a.m. - 9 p.m.

TYPE: Buffet, take-out and catering

PRICES: Buffet-average; Bulk rates-average

COOKING
TECHNIQUE: Open pit - oak and hickory

THE BARBECUE:

 From about 6 p.m. until closing time on Fridays and Saturdays, there is usually a long line of hungry, eager customers waiting to enter Oak Grove. It has been popular since 1960, when Mr. Roof opened his barbecue establishment. Now, though, the owner is the amiable Henry Dunn, who has been cooking barbecue for over fifteen years. A tremendous amount of labor is involved in using the old open pit technique. At Oak Grove four people are rquired to help in the process. Cooking for the two days, done on Thursday and Friday, requires 26 hogs. They are cooked for 12 hours and are turned and sauced once in the process. The chopped barbecue is served with some sauce mixed in. The large chunks of meat were not as flavorful as were the small pieces, which were moist and lean. Although a bit greasy and spare, the pork ribs (which always run out early at Oak Grove) had a noticeable wood smoke taste and a crunchy exterior. Well sauced and tender, the chicken displayed a pleasant smoked taste, especially in the crisp outer covering. On each table were several bottles of Dunn's Oak and Hickory Flavored Bar-B-Cue Table Sauce, which contain, among other ingredients, anchovies, tamirinds, mustard seed, and mustard bran. The sauce, which the customers may purchase for their own barbecuing and cooking needs, was pleasantly mild and not too heavy on the mustard taste. The hash, a pork and beef combination, was mildly seasoned. Also served on the all-you-can-eat buffet are salty pork skins, cole slaw, pickles, white loaf bread, tea, lemonade, and coffee. Tooth picks, hot pepper sauce, and pitchers of tea are on each table.

THE PLACE:

Probably the first thing one notices as he drives up to Oak Grove is the gigantic (about twenty feet high) pile of wood beside the restaurant. Inside a semi-enclosed metal and brick structure the wood is burned. When the coals have burned down, they are transfered to the two long open pits and covered with metal sheets to keep in heat and smoke. This pit room is a long, low, screened building that interested customers may peer into. Inside the dining room is seating for 140 (usually elbow-to-elbow) at long wooden tables covered with red and white oil cloths. Bamboo shades cover the windows, and photographs of people feasting on barbecue decorate some of the concrete walls. A take-out window is located at a side entrance to the building.

* * * * * * *

COWAN'S RANCH BAR-B-QUE

LOCATION: 2529 Millwood Avenue, Columbia 254-3079

HOURS: Mon.-Wed. 11 a.m. - 8 p.m.; Thurs. 11 a.m. - 10 p.m.; Fri.-Sat. 11 a.m. - 12 p.m.

TYPE: Regular menu, take-out and catering

PRICES: Dinners-average; Bulk rates-average

COOKING
TECHNIQUE: Closed pit - indirect heat and smoke from hickory

THE BARBECUE:

Oklahoman Joe Cowan opened Cowan's Ranch Bar-B-Que (specializing in Western-style barbecue) in February 1979. Few places in South Carolina serve beef (a Western specialty), and Cowan's is one of those places. For his pork barbecue he cooks shoulders and hams for 12-14 hours, watching them carefully, turning them occasionally, and mopping them with a seasoning sauce of vinegar, mustard and pepper. Cowan uses a unique method of cooking - one we have found only in two other places (Sawgrass Jim's in Spartanburg and David Brown's in Winnsboro). He places burning hickory coals in a separate compartment of a brick oven. The hickory smoke is drawn through the vents into the oven compartment and cooks (or cures) the meat slowly. This method allows the hickory flavor to permeate the meat thoroughly, resulting in some delicious barbecue.

Joe Cowan's special pork, chopped into large, lean chunks, had a good hickory flavor. One of his two mustard sauces (the sour one with a bite to it and plenty of vinegar or the milder, sweeter one) goes well with the pork. The meaty pork ribs were covered with a rich tomatoey sauce, and more of this sweet concoction may be added if the customer desires. The barbecued beef, which Cowan says is one of his most popular items and the most expensive to prepare, was of the tender, melt-in-your-mouth variety. Even the succulent chicken had a pleasant hickory-smoked aroma and taste. The hash, made with beef and pork, had a slight liver flavor to it. Cowan serves barbecue dinners, plates, sandwiches, and side orders of baked beans, peaches, cole slaw and potato salad. Those who have never tried smoke-cured meat should visit Cowan's and taste the flavor.

THE PLACE:

This tiny Western-decorated place has only two booths and two tables (seating for 12) but there's more room to stand.

* * * * * * *

MIDLAND KITCHEN

LOCATION: 5403 Forest Drive, Columbia 782-0688

HOURS: Mon.-Fri. 10:30 a.m. - 9 p.m. and Sat. 11 a.m. - 9 p.m.

TYPE: Regular menu, take-out and catering

PRICES: Dinners-low; Bulk rates-average

COOKING
TECHNIQUE: Electric cooked - then wood smoked in a separate compartment

THE BARBECUE:

Two and a half years ago, when the Midland Kitchen first opened, owner Harold Gayden served barbecued beef and chicken, in addition to pork. Because they didn't sell well, he dropped them from his menu, and now all his barbecue business is in chopped pork. Two separate processes are involved in cooking the pork. First, the dry-seasoned shoulders are cooked, fat-side up, in an electric oven for 12 hours. Then they are moved to another closed compartment where they are cured with hickory and oak smoke for 6 hours. A little sauce is mixed in after the meat has been chopped, but the large chunks still retain a pleasant smoked flavor. Hash at Midland Kitchen, served only Thursday through Friday, is made with pork and some beef, and onion juice is the key ingredient that provides the zesty flavor. Two types of sauces are prepared by the owner. One has a tomato base, sweetened with brown sugar. The other, mustard-based, has a tangy kick to it. Other menu items are chicken, cole slaw and sandwiches.

THE PLACE:

Midland Kitchen, housed in a former fast-food joint, offers its customers cleanliness, bright light and molded plastic booths that seat 34.

* * * * * * *

THE SHADY REST PARK

LOCATION: 1927 Heidt Street, Columbia 771-9615

HOURS: Mon.-Wed. 5 p.m.- 12 p.m.; Thurs. 4 p.m. - 2 a.m.; Fri. 12 p.m. - 6 a.m.; Sat. 1 p.m. - 12 a. m.

TYPE: Regular menu and take-out

PRICES: Dinners-low; Bulk rates-average

COOKING
TECHNIQUE: Open pit - oak, hickory and charcoal

THE BARBECUE:

The Shady Rest Park, a small restaurant near Allen University and Benedict College and frequented by many students, has been owned and run by Mary Golden for 31 years. She cooks pork shoulders and ribs for 8-12 hours on a screened-in pit over hard wood and charcoal. To make her chopped and sliced barbecue, Mrs. Golden cuts off a slab of pork from a cooked shoulder and fries it on a flat griddle. Then a generous amount of sauce is poured over each helping. The result was thick slices of fatty pork. Though somewhat greasy, they were quite crunchy on the outside. The sauce, a 30 year-old recipe, was thin and slightly vinegary. In addition, the fare includes hash and rice, a popular item for the Shady Rest's clientele. Sandwiches, fried chicken and seafood are also on the menu.

THE PLACE:

      Surrounded by oak and pecan trees, the Shady Rest Park looks much older than its 31 years. Loiterers lounge on parked cars and old wooden crates outside the ramshackle building. Inside, customers may perch on wobbly stools at a counter laden with jars of pickled eggs and pigs' feet. A few broken-down booths and four tables with classroom chairs are able to accommodate about 40 people. As a battered juke box belts out the latest soul and disco tunes, a greasy ceiling fan churns the murky air.

* * * * * * *

SMITH'S BAR-B-QUE

LOCATION:	1801 Standish Rd. (off Farrow Rd.) Columbia 754-9850
HOURS:	Fri.-Sat. 9 a.m. - 10 p.m.
TYPE:	Take-out and catering
PRICES:	Bulk rates-average
COOKING TECHNIQUE:	Open pit - charcoal and sometimes hickory

THE BARBECUE:

      Sargeant R. Smith (retired U.S. Army) has operated Smith's Bar-B-Que for eighteen years. The manager, Sam West, explained that the pork shoulders, which are used for the chopped barbecue, are cooked on a long open pit over charcoal for twelve hours. Corrugated paper covers the meat to keep in heat and flavor. Smith's also offers ribs, chicken and hash. Sometimes after a successful hunting expedition, the employees will barbecue ducks, rabbits, or other game. Even turkeys are cooked occasionally. The stringy pork barbecue, lean, moist and flavorful, was accompanied by a mild mustard sauce. The pork skins were hot and crisp.

THE PLACE:

      This old cement-block building has screened windows almost all the way around it. On one end is a brick fireplace where the charcoal is started. The interior is completed with one long pit, one small one for warming, and wooden counter where the barbecue is weighed and sold.

* * * * * * *

THE PIT

LOCATION: 5740 Farrow Rd. (off Cushman Drive)
Columbia   786-8459

HOURS: Mon.-Thurs. 11:30 a.m. - 2 a.m.;
Fri.-Sat. 11 a.m. - 4 a.m.

TYPE: Regular menu, take-out and catering

PRICES: Dinners-average; Bulk rates-average

COOKING
TECHNIQUE: Electric

THE BARBECUE:

When George and JoAnn Jones opened The Pit in 1973, they used wood to cook their barbecue, but now they use electricity. Only shoulders, cooked unturned for 4 to 5-1/2 hours, are used to make their chopped barbecue. One thin sauce, which contains eleven ingredients and has a sweet, vinegar taste, is served with the meat. The chopped barbecue was a little sweet and fatty. The pork ribs were small, but very meaty and tender. The well-seasoned chicken was tender to the "falling-off-the-bone" point. Two other barbecue items are barbecued beef and hash. Served with the reasonably priced chopped barbecue dinner are hash and rice, cole slaw, and rolls. Plenty of sandwiches and non-barbecue items are also part of The Pit's fare.

THE PLACE:

The Pit consists of two connecting rooms with a juke box in each. Plastic tables and chairs and a counter with stools seat 84 customers. A few dusty Christmas decorations still adorn the walls in June. Tacked to the back wall is a dingy menu with out-of-date prices. Stacked neatly at the back of the small bar are rows of mini-bottles for those customers desiring something stronger than soft drinks or beer with their barbecue.

* * * * * * *

MULDROW'S BAR-B-QUE

LOCATION: 201 Bush River Rd. (near Boozer Shopping Center), Columbia   772-9065

HOURS: Mon.-Thurs. 11 a.m. - 9 p.m.; Fri.-Sat. 11 a.m. - 10 p.m.

TYPE: Regular menu, take-out, drive-up window and catering

PRICES: Dinners-average; Bulk rates-average

COOKING
TECHNIQUE: Electric

THE BARBECUE:

Although Bobby Muldrow has been cooking barbecue for years, Muldrow's Bar-B-Que has been open only since January 1979. Muldrow cooks hams and shoulders about 12 hours on an electric pit to make his chopped barbecue and his pork hash. The meat is seasoned lightly while cooking and sauced after it is chopped. Consisting of large, moist chunks of tender pork, the chopped barbecue had a delicious flavor that was accented by the sauce (a tangy mixture of tomato and mustard). The pork hash was mildly seasoned -- definitely not too spicy. Besides barbecue, Muldrow's offers a variety of hot dogs.

THE PLACE:

Muldrow's, located in an old fast-food establishment, still contains the original decor and atmosphere: bright yellow and orange interior, a walk-up order counter, and seating for 38 in molded plastic booths.

* * * * * * *

PORKY'S BAR-B-Q

LOCATION: 1202 Main St., Columbia   765-0410

HOURS: Mon.-Sat. 7:30 a.m. - 9 p.m.

TYPE: Regular menu and take-out

PRICES: Dinners-average; Bulk rates-high

COOKING
TECHNIQUE: Electric cooker - hickory-smoked.

THE BARBECUE:

    Porky's Bar-B-Q originated in Columbia in late March 1979. According to manager Champ McGee, who worked at the Little Barbecue Hut in the Rosewood Shopping Center before it burned down in August 1979, the members of Porky's, Inc., hope to franchise their fast-food operation in other South Carolina cities soon. Porky's serves two types of barbecued meat: chopped or sliced pork and ribs. Champ McGee, with thirteen years of barbecue cooking on which to rely, has brought his own ideas and techniques to Porky's. During the last two hours of the twelve hours of the cooking process, the pork shoulders are smoked with hickory chips. Then they are sauced and put back into the Kookrite electric pit and hickory-smoked for another six hours. The chopped pork, which should be called minced because it is so finely cut, had a light hickory flavor. Although quite lean, the meat was a little greasy. The chunk barbecue had a more distinct flavor of hickory and a little sweeter taste, perhaps from the sauce. The ribs, though small, were meaty with a well-cooked, chewy exterior and a hickory taste. Three types of sauces are served with the barbecue: a mild, thick sauce with a slightly sweet flavor; a hot one; and a sharp mustard-based one. Specialites include hash (made with 2/3 beef and 1/3 pork), hot dogs, potato wheels (somewhere between hash browns and french fries), and Champ's recipe for barbecued baked beans (hickory-smoked, just as the meat is). Barbecue dinners are accompanied by slaw, hush puppies, and baked beans.

THE PLACE:

    The bright blue exterior with its blue and white striped awning and old-fashioned ceiling fan serves as a pleasant welcome to the place. Inside, the customer is greeted by royal blue formica-topped tables and pink padded chairs. The pink and blue color scheme is repeated in the smiling pink faces of Porky Pigs on the powder blue walls. Imitation wood grained booths and narrow counters with stools line the walls. Tables, booths, and counters can accommodate 75. At the rear of the restaurant, separating the kitchen from the dining area, is a walk-up counter where the customer places his order. Nearby stands a three-barrel table that holds several chili kettles.

****

THE BAR-B-QUERY - J.D. HITE AND SON

LOCATION: 240 Dreher Rd. (off U.S. 1) West Columbia   794-4120

HOURS: Fri. 9 a.m. - 8 p.m. and Sat. 8 a.m. - 7 p.m.

TYPE: Take-out only

PRICES: Bulk rates-average

COOKING TECHNIQUE: Open pit - oak and hickory

THE BARBECUE:

Mr. J.D. Hite started The Bar-B-Query, which serves only carry-out orders, 30 years ago. When he died, his son and daughter-in-law, Jerry Wayne and Brenda Hite, took over the operation. The Hites cook at least 500 pounds of meat per week over hickory and oak coals. During the 12 hour cooking process, the hogs are basted with a mustard sauce and turned once. Their barbecue offerings consist of chopped pork, ribs, chicken, and skin. Other specialities include ham (no sauce) and beef/pork hash. The chopped barbecue was lean and moist. There was little evidence of smoked flavor, but a thin, mild mustard sauce (which the customer may purchase by the pint) added some flavor to the meat. The pork ribs were meaty and juicy.

THE PLACE:

The cement block building is slightly off the beaten path and easy to miss if you drive too fast. A simple counter separates the customer from the barbecue operation. Prices are posted on the wall.

* * * * * * *

OKRA PATCH

LOCATION: Hwy. 60 (Newberry Hwy.), Irmo 781-2247.

HOURS: Mon. - Wed. 8 a.m. - 7 p.m.;
                Thurs. - Sat. 8 a.m. - 9 p.m.

TYPE: Regular menu and take-out.

PRICES: Dinners-low; Bulk rates - average.

COOKING
TECHNIQUE: Closed brick pit - oak and hickory.

THE BARBECUE:

          The Okra Patch, called Lorick's Barbecue for the past twenty-seven years, relies on black-jack oak and hickory to cook their shoulders and hams. The meat is turned once after it has cooked for 6 or 7 hours. After cooking another 4 hours, the pork is chopped and sauced. Served by the pound, buffet plates, and in sandwiches, the chopped barbecue consists of small chunks of pork in an almost undetectable mustard-based sauce. Hash and beef stew are two other specialities at the Okra Patch. The menu also includes non-barbecue entrees.

THE PLACE:

          Located on a winding, tree-lined road, the grey, wood-shingled building contains bright orange booths (40-50 seating capacity) and walls, pinball machines, and a juke box filled with country music selections.

-32-

* * * * * * *

SAM'S BAR-B-Q

LOCATION: 7130 Fairfield Rd. (Hw. 321 North of I-20 interchange) Columbia

HOURS: Serving barbecue Fri.-Sat. 7 a.m. - 8 p.m.; serving other food Mon.-Sat. 7 a.m. - 8 p.m.

TYPE: Take-out only

PRICES: Bulk rates-average

COOKING
TECHNIQUE: Closed pit - charcoal

THE BARBECUE:

    Arthur "Sam" Samuel has been selling his barbecue over the sandwich counter of his small grocery on Hwy. 321 for over 29 years. The robust fifty-one-year-old cooks his pork in a small metal oven over charcoal. Twelve hours are spent cooking the hams, and the pork is turned at the halfway point. After the pork has been thoroughly cooked, Samuel bastes the pork with his own mustard-based sauce. He serves the meat chopped or sliced, offering his customers a barbecue that has a strong charcoal taste. The barbecued pork had a minimal amount of fat, and the tangy, mustard-based sauce accented the rich smoke flavor. Sandwich portions are generous, and Samuel's menu includes a respectable tasting beef hash with a rich, oniony taste. Although Sam's serves barbecue only on Fridays and Saturdays, the restaurant offers a complete sandwich menu and non-barbecue items six days a week.

THE PLACE:

    Sam's is an overstuffed, quick-stop grocery with a sandwich counter tucked away in one corner of the building. Amidst sundry items, Sam's serves his pork specialties to barbecue hungry motorists and truckers who happen by the tiny establishment.

* * * * * * *

SIKE'S BAR-B-Q

LOCATION: 14 miles east of Columbia's Va Hospital on Hwy. 378, Eastover 353-9620

HOURS: Thurs.-Sat. 10 a.m. - 10 p.m.

TYPE: Regular menu, buffet, take-out and catering

PRICES: Buffet-average; dinner-average; bulk rates-average

COOKING
TECHNIQUE: Open pit - charcoal

THE BARBECUE:

    Owners Allen Sikes and his son Bubber have operated their barbecue business since 1967. For the first 4 or 5 years they used hard wood to cook their meat, but now they use charcoal in a large cement pit. Wednesday, Thursday, and Friday are their cooking days; they cook pork hams for 16-17 hours, turning them occasionally. After the pork is chopped, it is mixed with a tangy, mustard-based sauce. The pork barbecue is served two ways: minced and sliced. (Sliced pork is a rarity in many areas of South Carolina with the exception of the northwestern part, around Spartanburg and Greenville). Both types had a distinct charcoal flavor, and the sauce that is mixed in with the minced barbecue accented - rather than overcame - the pork taste. Barbecued chicken and pork hash are also popular at Sikes'. The buffet is all-you-can-eat only if the customer orders a large plate, consisting of pork, hash, rice, and slaw. Employees, not the customers, help the plates.

THE PLACE:

    Located in a white cement-block building connected to an Exxon station, Sikes' Bar-B-Q is a well-packed, well-worn establishment with a friendly atmosphere. The eating area contains old booths and tables for four, seating 50-60. Scattered throughout are displays of merchandise that make Sikes' resemble an old country store. A jolly fat pig dressed in top hat and cane decorates a large sign near the Sumter Highway.

* * * * * * *

RAY LEVER'S BAR-B-Q HUT

LOCATION: 6 miles north of I-20 between Hwy. 21 and Hwy. 321 on Lorick Rd., Blythewood
754-8408 (day) or 754-3496 (night)

HOURS: Thurs.-Sun. 11 a.m. - 9:45 p.m.

TYPE: Buffet, take-out and catering

PRICES: Buffet-average; Bulk rates-average

COOKING
TECHNIQUE: Open pit - hickory

THE BARBECUE:

Opened twelve years ago, Ray Lever's Bar-B-Q Hut suffered a devastating pit fire on July 4, 1971. During the two weeks of repairs, significant changes in the construction were made. Two of those changes included raising considerably the height of the ceiling in the screened pit room and using metal, instead of wood, for the ceiling beams. One long metal pit runs the length of the building. Beside it are gigantic steel kettles where the hash is simmered and an electric barbecue pit. The Levers cook shoulders (for their chopped barbecue) and ribs over hickory that is started in a separate area near the pit. The lean barbecue, chopped into large chunks, had a light vinegar taste, but there was little evidence of any smoke flavor. Although quite meaty, the ribs had very little flavor -- sauce or otherwise. However, the beef hash made our visit to Lever's worthwhile. Served over rice, it was spicy, oniony, and quite tasty.

To accompany the meat, Ray Lever's offers four types of sauces, which the owner prepares and bottles in an area behind the kitchen and then sells commercially. The mopping (or basting) sauce, made to be used during the cooking of the pork, tasted like pure mustard with a few spices thrown in. The mustard-based sauce was not as mustardy as the mopping sauce, but neither was it tangy or spicy. The ketchup-based sauce had a strange taste (very unlike ketchup) that is difficult to describe. The hot sauce definitely lived up to its name. Accompanying the barbecued meat on the all-you-can-eat buffet were two kinds of hush puppies, baked beans, slaw, potato salad, corn on the cob, crisp pork skins, pickles, white loaf bread and iced tea.

THE PLACE:

      Both dining rooms (the newer opened in August 1979) contain stainless steel buffet set-ups and typical school cafeteria-style seating (long folding tables and metal chairs). The windowless walls are rather stark, especially with the effect of bright fluorescent lighting and white stucco ceilings. Several hundred people can be accommodated in both dining rooms.

                    * * * * * * *

WARD'S BAR-B-Q

LOCATION: 2-1/2 miles from Columbia's VA Hospital on Highway 378 783-2548
Thurs.-Sat. 10:30 a.m. - 7:30 p.m.

See Ward's Bar-B-Q, Sumter, on page 103.

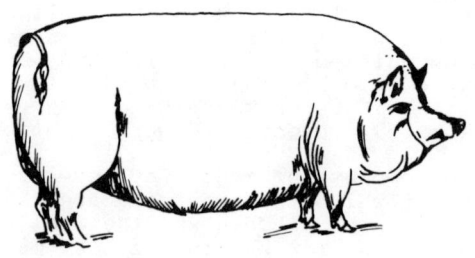

****

SOUTHEAST REGION

****

SWEATMAN'S BAR-B-QUE

LOCATION:	Hwy. 453 between Holly Hill and Eutawville
HOURS:	Fri.-Sat. 11:30 a.m. - 10:30 p.m.
TYPE:	Buffet, take-out and catering.
PRICES:	Buffet-low; dinners-low
COOKING TECHNIQUE:	Open pit - oak

THE BARBECUE:

    Barbecuing is a 3-generation tradition for H.O. "Bub" Sweatman and his family. Seventy-five years ago the Sweatmans were digging pits in their back yard, barbecuing pigs, and asking friends over to partake in the feast. The tradition continued for years, with the friends helping defray costs by chipping in whatever they thought the food was worth. For 5 or 6 years Sweatman had a barbecue every Saturday in Holly Hill, and there developed such a demand for it that in October 1977 he bought a 75 or 80-year-old farm house between Holly Hill and Eutawville and began cooking barbecue every Friday and Saturday.

    Out back on a concrete slab under a semi-shelter, oak limbs are cut up and burned. When the coals are ready they are brought into the screened room and deposited in a long cement pit through heavy metal doors on the side. Whole hogs (about 15-20 per weekend) are placed on metal grills above the coal bed. After 5 or 6 hours, sauce is applied and the basting is frequent for the next 5 or 6 hours.

    The careful preparations are not in vain. Sweatman's barbecue feast is hard to beat in all ways: quality, taste, variety, and price. Saying that something is the "best" always gives people a chance to say, "But what about ---------?" or "Have you tried -- -----------?" So, perhaps it's best to leave it at this: For barbecue, Sweatman's ranks number one in this area and in the top five places of the state. That's a safe claim - one very few people should take exception to.

Bub Sweatman serves generous-sized chunks of pork that are bursting with hickory flavor. The lean, juicy meat almost melted in the mouth. With a dash of the slightly sweet and spicy mustard sauce (a 75 year-old recipe), the pork flavor is accented, not obscured. Sweatman gives his customers a hand by removing some of the rib meat from the bones and serving it minus the ribs. But for those who enjoy gnawing on the bones and sucking every drop of sauce from them, there is a supply of meaty ribs, too. Only a few barbecue establishments come close to preparing ribs the way Sweatman does. The chewy ribs, basted with a light tomato and spice sauce, were a delectable delight. Even the tender meat of the chicken, well-sauced on the outside with the spicy tomato mixture, had a delicate smoked flavor. Pork hash, a favorite of many of the locals, was a mild, tomatoey concoction. Although a little greasy, the pork skins were fried to a thin, crisp lightness. The additions to the Sweatman buffet are few, because the customers come for one reason: his barbecue. The rest of the buffet consists of dill pickles, cole slaw, white loaf bread or rolls, and iced tea. The buffet, once an all-you-can-eat affair, is now an all-you-can-eat-in-one-serving affair. One can fill a large plate, eat it all, and not go away hungry.

THE PLACE:

The setting of Sweatman's gourmet barbecue is idyllic: Giant pecan trees shade the weathered farmhouse-turned feasting place. A wide porch, whose floor boards have been blanched and worn by hot sun and pounding rains, stretches across the front of the shingled house. Fertile farmland, alive with young plants, extends for many acres beside the old house.

Inside, ceiling-paneling covers the walls of the five dining rooms (once bedrooms and living areas) and reaches up to and covers the 12 feet high ceilings. Some of the walls are adorned with landscapes and other paintings. Fireplaces in four of the dining rooms add a touch of warmth, as do the gingham and patchwork curtains on the screened windows. Seating for 80 is provided at picnic tables with benches and at metal tables with straight-back chairs. The oil cloths and the scattered country decorations provide the final "homey" touch for a comfortable trip back to the 1900's.

* * * * * * *

BESSINGER'S BARBECUE HOUSE

LOCATION: 1) Hwy. 17 South, in Charleston 556-1354
               2) 114 Doughty St. Charleston 723-2241

HOURS: Mon.-Thurs. 11 a.m. - 7 p.m.;
               Fri.-Sat. 11 a.m. - 11 p.m.

TYPE: Regular menu, buffet, take-out, drive-in and catering

PRICES: Buffet-average; dinners-average; bulk rates-average-high

COOKING
TECHNIQUE: Open pit - hickory

THE BARBECUE:

Bessinger may be the biggest name in barbecue in South Carolina, and nowhere is this more evident than in Charleston, where Melvin and Tommy Bessinger have the most industrious enterprise we've seen. The Bessinger's location on Hwy. 17 South offers tourists and town-folk a taste of real open-pit barbecue at its best. In the 1930's, when Joe Bessinger opened a tiny cafe in Holly Hill, he couldn't have dreamed that the sauce recipe he handed down to his children would enjoy the widespread popularity it does today. Bessinger's Charleston-based sons would have made their father proud with what they've turned that sauce recipe into: a three-location food enterprise that enjoys a booming trade. The Bessinger boys believe in cooking pork right. Their open-pit hickory-smoked pork and ribs are served with the mustard-based sauce that wears the Bessinger name. The finely chopped, somewhat chewy pork barbecue had a rich, smoked taste. Ribs were meaty, overly crisped on the outside, and very juicy next to the bone. Besides barbecue, Bessinger's offers seafood entrees, a full sandwich menu, and desserts. Dinners include cole slaw, hash over rice, and a hot roll. The buffet offers a similar spread. Seven out of eleven Bessinger children are involved in the restaurant business, and, as brother Melvin Bessinger was once said to have remarked, "I've never seen a lazy Bessinger." That idea is carried through by the employees in the Bessinger restaurants. They are a cheerful, industrious group who work at a break-neck pace to keep their customers satisfied. Bessinger's barbecue is also served at Market Square. The unique surroundings deserved special attention. (See separate listing in the directory.

THE PLACE:

The Bessinger's location on Hwy. 17 sets the pace for the other locations. The restaurant features a rustic, busy atmosphere both inside and out. A drive-in area on the far side of the parking lot is usually full of cars. The curb service is quick and many people take advantage of the convenience of car-served barbecue. The entire left side of the Bessinger location is devoted to the buffet area where over 100 hungry customers can help themselves to a full line of barbecue treats. With a huge kitchen area situated in the center section of the building, the restaurant is divided so that the right end of the building is devoted to the Bessinger sandwich shop. Customers in this section can order a light meal, dinner, or a take-out sampling of Bessinger's pit-cooked barbecue. For fast service, clean surroundings, and employees who are eager to please, Bessinger's is hard to beat.

* * * * * * *

BESSINGER'S BAR-B-Q

LOCATION: Market Square, Market St. off East Bay
                St., Charleston   577-9409

HOURS: Mon.-Sat. 11 a.m. - 7 p.m.

TYPE: Regular menu and take-out

PRICES: Dinners-high; bulk rates-high

COOKING
TECHNIQUE: Open pit - wood

THE BARBECUE:

The really nice thing about this location is that it allows non-barbecue lovers from your eating party to choose from a dozen other quick-service food facilities. Located in the Market Square food emporium, Bessinger's (for owner profile, see Bessinger's Bar-B-Q Hwy. 17 location in Charleston entry) offers one of the best quick-stop barbecues to be found in South Carolina. Despite the fact that the meat is prepared away from the sales point, the food here is better than the menu offerings at many of the barbecue restaurants located right beside their pits.

The finely chopped pork barbecue, juicy and somewhat chewy, had a smoky, well-cooked taste that was complimented by the spicy sauce. The mustard-based sauce finds its way onto other barbecue items on the menu and can be purchased by the pint for home use. Beef barbecue was a salty tasting offering at Bessinger's that did not stand up to the pork in comparison. Ribs were meaty, crisp on the outside, and lean and juicy next to the bone. Tourists in Charleston will appreciate the convenient location of a true South Carolina barbecue restaurant and will be served a respectable version of this traditional Southern dish.

THE PLACE:

An open, sheltered dining area provides seating for the eating establishments in Market Square. The walk-up counter for Bessinger's is located beneath a rustic wood facade bearing the Bessinger name in bold, bright letters. While the barbecue lovers of the family enjoy Melvin and Tommy Bessinger's barbecue items, other members can choose from such foods as pizza, seafood or submarine sandwiches at some of the many restaurants surrounding the open dining area, which can accommodate about 200 patrons.

* * * * * * *

PIGGY PARK

LOCATION: 23 Coleman Rd. (Hwy. 17 & 703), Mt. Pleasant
884-3306

HOURS: Mon.-Sat. 11 a.m. - 6 p.m.

TYPE: Take-out only

PRICES: Dinners-low; bulk rates-average

COOKING
TECHNIQUE: Gas

THE BARBECUE:

For quick service, J.D. Bessinger's Piggy Park is second to none. Piggy Park is a quick stop sandwich shop, but their specialty is barbecue. That barbecue is served smothered in a mustard-based sauce that tends to disguise, rather than distinguish, the meat. The sauce, when administered in reasonable doses, is probably one of the better mild, mustard-based sauces in the region, but it is served at Piggy Park with a heavy hand.

THE PLACE:

Packed between gas stations and quick shops, Piggy Park is a flat-topped, cream colored restaurant that allows motorists fast service on a wide variety of grill items. Customers place their orders at a walk-up window and wait outside while the orders are being filled.

* * * * * * *

KEITH'S RED BARN

LOCATION: 103 Edgewood St., Walterboro   549-5141

HOURS: Mon.-Sun. 11 a.m. - 9 p.m.

TYPE: Regular menu, take-out and catering. Keith's was formerly buffet, but switched to regular menu to standardize Keith's restaurants throughout the chain

PRICES: Dinners-average; bulk rates-average

COOKING
TECHNIQUE: Electric-cooked chopped pork/charcoal-cooked ribs and chickens

THE BARBECUE:

W. L. Keith started selling barbecue over 31 years ago as a sideline to his grocery business. Today Keith's sons, Wayne, Lewis, and Lenny, have taken control of the operation and it is fast becoming a leading barbecue wholesale operation. Barbecue for all Keith's locations is cooked one of two ways. Chopped pork is prepared at the wholesale preparation plant. Electric cookers are used to their capacity and potential when the Keith's people prepare the food for their three locations. They have managed to take a large scale approach to the barbecue business without relinquishing the personalized quality of the pork cooking. The chopped pork offered on the menu was a finely chopped, moist, and tender pork barbecue - ranking it in the upper echelons of electric-cooked meat. Keith's manages consistency in taste, regardless of which Keith's location you choose to visit. The brick charcoal pits found in each location are used to prepare meaty (though somewhat bland) ribs and tender, juicy barbecued chickens. Keith's hash is a pork/chicken blend that includes potatoes, onions, and tomatoes in this unique recipe. Keith's strives for quality and taste in every meal they prepare.

THE PLACE:

Keith's rambling red barn is the birthplace of a rapidly expanding chain of restaurants. The restaurant seats close to 100 customers in a dining area designed for comfort. The original Keith's location is located near the wholesale plant/headquarters for the chain. The facility is always busy preparing chopped pork for faraway cities in Maryland and New York. The industrious Keith brothers are hard at work building their own barbecue dynasty.

* * * * * * *

KEITH'S BARBECUE

LOCATION: 6141 Rivers Ave. (Hwy. 52/78) in North Charleston 797-1070

HOURS: Every day 11 a.m. - 9 p.m.

TYPE: Regular menu, take-out, and catering

PRICES: Dinners-average; bulk rates-average

COOKING TECHNIQUE: Electric-cooked chopped pork and charcoal-cooked ribs and chicken

THE BARBECUE:

See "Keith's Red Barn" entry for Walterboro.

THE PLACE:

The Keith's Rivers Ave. location is an exercise in the standardization movement being incorporated by the rapidly expanding Walterboro firm. Borrowing from the restaurant formula of franchise operations, Keith's barbecue is served in sterile surroundings that are reminiscent of fast-food restaurants. This Keith's location seats approximately 75 people.

* * * * * * *

RAST'S RESTAURANT

LOCATION: Bohicket Rd., John's Island -- 16 miles from Charleston and 9 miles from Kiawah Island 559-0006

HOURS: Mon. 12 p.m. - 5 p.m. and Tues.-Sun. 12 p.m. - 10:30 p.m.

TYPE: Regular menu

PRICES: Dinners-high

COOKING TECHNIQUE: Combination gas/charcoal (PDQ Cooker)

THE BARBECUE:

Although owner Henry Rast has been cooking barbecue all his life, he has been cooking it commercially for only 6-7 years. Manager Ray Balzano explained that the pork shoulders for the chopped barbecue are cooked slowly on medium heat (gas) for about 5-1/2 hours. Then the meat is taken off the bone, chopped, mixed with a mustard-based sauce, and set back in the cooker for another hour while the flavor "sets". The chicken and ribs are cooked with indirect heat from the charcoal on Rast's own patented PDQ (Pretty Darn Quick) Cooker. The chopped barbecue was quite lean and lightly seasoned. Accenting the flavor was the sauce, whose special ingredient (pineapple juice) gave it a little different taste than most mustard-based sauces. Both the hot, juicy ribs and the meaty, well-seasoned chicken had a garlic butter flavor, giving the meat an unusual but pleasant taste. Neither the ribs nor the chicken was basted in a barbecue sauce while cooking.

House specialties include fresh seafood (especially soft-shelled crabs), charcoal onions (cooked with butter and honey), fresh vegetables from Mrs. Rast's garden, Pilau hash and rice, and sweet cornbread. The menu includes a variety of non-barbecue entrees, also. Although priced a little high, the dinners are bountifully accompanied by home-cooked garden vegetables that make the price well worth it. The Barbecue Platter, for instance, consists of pork, ribs, chicken, hash Pilau and rice, vegetables, pickles, cole slaw, and french bread or cornbread. Only those serious about eating should attempt this feast.

THE PLACE:

Surrounded by lush vegetation and overlooking a marshy creek, Rast's Restaurant is a large, open building decorated with wildlife (stuffed fish, geese, deer). There are plenty of large tables to accommodate about 140 customers. One room off to the side (the PDQ Room) is devoted to displaying Rast's patented cooking apparatus and to explaining the history behind its development. Efficient, friendly waitresses serve the clientele well and do not hesitate to explain specialty items on the menu or to give advice about crabbing in the creek.

* * * * * * *

KEITH'S BARBECUE

LOCATION: Beaufort Plaza Shopping Mall on Hwy. 21, Beaufort   524-8171

HOURS: Every day 11 a.m. - 9 p.m.

TYPE: Regular menu, take-out and catering

PRICES: Dinners-average; bulk rates-average

COOKING TECHNIQUE: Electric-cooked chopped pork and charcoal-cooked ribs and chicken

THE BARBECUE:

See "Keith's Red Barn" entry for Walterboro.

THE PLACE:

This Keith's restaurant gives customers very little feel for the traditional elements associated with barbecue. Gone are the folding tables, benches, and loaves of white bread. Keith's has a sophisticated atmosphere that tends to take some of the romance out of the barbecue eating experience. The restaurant can accommodate 100.

* * * * * * *

LESTER'S PIT BAR-B-Q

LOCATION:	5 miles east of Estill and 9 miles south of Hampton on Hwy. 601 625-2305
HOURS:	Thurs.-Sat. 10 a.m. - 9 p.m.
TYPE:	Buffet, take-out, drive-up window service and catering
PRICES:	Buffet-average; dinners-average; bulk rates-average
COOKING TECHNIQUE:	Open pit - charcoal

THE BARBECUE:

"I just decided I was tired of working for another man." That's what convinced Lester DeLoach to pick a spot outside Hampton and build an open pit barbecue house. Lester's all-you-can-eat buffet is a clean and simple operation. He serves pork-rice, pilau, turnip greens, cole slaw, homemade pickles and loaf bread with his chopped or sliced pork. During the slow-cooking on his open pit, the pork is salted but never sauced. The meat is served coarsely chopped or sliced, and Lester DeLoach offers customers a choice between two kinds of sauce: a mustard/lemon juice/spicy hot sauce or a mustard/ketchup/slightly peppered sauce that is quite a bit milder. DeLoach's barbecue was somewhat chewy and had just a trace of smoked taste. Combined with either of the sauces, Lester's barbecue was typical of pit-cooked pork entrees found in the barbecue rich regions of the state.

THE PLACE:

Set back from the highway on a lonely stretch of Hwy. 601, Lester's Bar-B-Q would look like a rural residence if it were not for the paved parking lot and the tall post (bearing Lester's name vertically) situated near the road. The well-scrubbed (inside and out), white building features a drive-up window off to one side. The dining room can seat over 40 people at formica-covered picnic tables. The walls in Lester's are adorned with photographs of "pork parties" DeLoach has thrown from time to time, and the view past the buffet area gives diners a glimpse of an exceptionally clean kitchen. Lester's strives for cleanliness in appearance and attitude. A sign hanging over the buffet asks customers the question "Have you thanked Him today?"

* * * * * * *

FENNELL'S BAR-B-Q

LOCATION: Near the city limits on Hwy. 363, just east of Hampton 943-4632

HOURS: Wed.-Sat. 10 a.m. - 9:30 p.m.

TYPE: Buffet, take-out and catering

PRICES: Buffet-average; Dinners-average; bulk rates-average

COOKING
TECHNIQUE: Closed pit - charcoal

THE BARBECUE:

As if farming 140 acres of rich lowcountry farm land weren't enough work for a man, Billy Fennell made the decision seven years ago to venture into the barbecue business. Now, along with nurturing the growth of his soy bean, corn, and melon crops, Fennell spends long hours and pit-smoked nights tending to his barbecue enterprise. Fennell cooks whole hogs for 9 hours over a thick, even layer of charcoal to produce what he calls "...a more flavorful meat." His barbecued pork was finely chopped, lean, and just a bit dry. Cooking over charcoal gives his barbecue a deep smoked taste that electric pit users seem to have a hard time matching -- even when they use a smoke box.

Fennell serves two kinds of sauces in his restaurant, both of which were developed by his mother, Aleane Fennell, who still works in the business with him. The Fennell hot sauce was a watery, vinegar-based blend of peppery spices that had a sharp taste. The mild sauce was a pretty standard blend of ketchup, sugar, and spices. Pork ribs were meaty, well-crisped offerings on the buffet menu, and Mrs. Fennell's hash recipe (her secret) includes pork and several different vegetables. Pork skins, and oven-baked, basted chickens complete the all-you-can-eat buffet.

THE PLACE

When Billy Fennell decided to go into the barbecue business, he went all the way. Fennell's Bar-B-Q is housed in a seven year-old building (built expressly for this business) that features dark wood paneling, indirect flourescent lighting, plenty of windows, and cheerful wall hangings. Pictures, simple free-hanging curtains and decorative heavy roping break the monotony of the dark walls. Customers are at the buffet as soon as they enter the front door. After filling their plates, they are free to select a place at any of the folding tables and chairs that are squeezed into the tiny dining room. The room can accommodate 50-55 customers.

* * * * * * *

DUKE'S BBQ

LOCATION: 435 Parler Ave., St. George   563-3939

     Harry Ott opens this restaurant on a seasonal schedule using the same menu and cooking methods employed at his "Duke's" location in Orangeburg. See the "Duke's BBQ-Chestnut St." entry for descriptions and prices.

* * * * * * *

DROZES BAR-B-Q

LOCATION: Hwy. 78, 1/2 mile east of Summerville   873-044

HOURS: Thurs.-Sat. 11 a.m. - 8:30 p.m.

TYPE: Buffet, take-out and catering

PRICES: Buffet-low; dinners-low; bulk rates-average

COOKING
TECHNIQUE: Open pit - charcoal

THE BARBECUE:

     Lee Droze is the soft-spoken, overly modest owner of one of Summerville's several successful barbecue businesses. In only a few short years, Droze has established himself as one of the barbecue experts in an area of the state that already has some notable barbecue barons. Demand for Droze's barbecue is such that he must prepare 1,000-1,500 pounds of pork per week to meet the needs of customers who visit one of his two locations. Using only shoulders and hams, Droze lets the meat cook 8-12 hours, depending on the size of the portions. To ensure thoroughly cooked pork, he turns the meat late in the cooking process. The pork is then chopped, and Droze applies a vinegar/ketchup/spice sauce which, he says, gives the pork its rich barbecue taste. The result is a lean, finely chopped barbecue that had a slight charcoal flavor. One can almost taste the hours of cooking that went into the preparation of the meat. Droze's table sauce (available for take-out customers to purchase) must be applied sparingly to avoid destroying the rich taste of the pork. The sauce is a very hot vinegar/pepper mixture that will accent the smoked flavor of the meat if used lightly. Droze balances his all-you-can-eat buffet menu with pork hash (a respectable hash), cole slaw (a tangy, vinegar mixture), and pork skins. Customers may help themselves to plenty of white loaf bread and iced tea at their tables.

THE PLACE:

Cleanliness is the key word from Lee Droze. He offers his customers the chance to enjoy barbecued pork in a well-lighted, sparkling white dining area that can easily seat over 100 people. Booths and tables are placed at close but comfortable distances to ensure the customer easy access to the bountiful buffet. Patrons will recognize Drozes as a long, low, structure on their left as they head east out of Summerville on Hwy. 78. Lee Droze has his entire family involved in the preparation and serving of this truly delicious barbecue.

* * * * * * *

DUKE'S BBQ

LOCATION: 789 Chestnut St. (Hwy. 21) on the north side of Orangeburg 534-9418

HOURS: Thurs.-Sat. 11 a.m. - 2 p.m. and 5 p.m. - 9 p.m.

TYPE: Buffet and take-out

PRICES: Buffet-low; bulk rates-average

COOKING TECHNIQUE: Gas

THE BARBECUE:

Harry Ott, at age 34, has been close to the barbecue business for 26 years. Having apprenticed near open pits with various members of his family, he learned his lessons well. Four years ago Ott brought his brand of barbecue to Orangeburg as an offshoot to his mother's barbecue business. Today Ott serves a lean, chopped version of barbecue. He cooks whole hogs over 11 hours on a gas pit to achieve a mouth-watering pork barbecue. The meat is chopped in an open kitchen area as customer demand necessitates, so those same patrons can witness the preparation of the choice portions of pork. Ott applies no sauce to the pork during preparation, but supplies his customers with a sweet, mild table sauce (also available for take-out) made from ketchup, mustard, sugar, and salad dressing. Unsauced, the barbecue had a richly cooked taste. Portions were moist and flaky. With the addition of sauce the rich pork taste was highlighted - not overpowered. Ott's hash was an oniony rendering. To complete the all-you-can-eat buffet Ott includes slaw, pickles, rice, loaf bread, and plenty of iced tea.

THE PLACE:

Duke's is a huge, cement-block building perched on the edge of northbound Hwy. 21 at the edge of Orangeburg. Over 100 customers can be served, and every table offers ample helpings of the traditional white bread and iced tea that are as much a part of barbecue tradition as the cooked meat. Ott's barbecue is served in clean, stark surroundings. Harry and his wife are an industrious pair who are quick to point out that they will "bend over backward to keep you happy."

* * * * * * *

DUKE'S BAR-B-Q

LOCATION:	1298 Whitman St. (1 block from Hwy. 301), Orangeburg 534-2916
HOURS:	Thurs.-Sat. 11 a.m. - 9 p.m.
TYPE:	Buffet and take-out
PRICES:	Buffet-average; bulk rates-average
COOKING TECHNIQUE:	Gas

THE BARBECUE:

The taciturn nature of the owners prevented any profile of this establishment from being written. The all-you-can-eat buffet features the traditional barbecue items, including chopped pork, hash and rice, pickles, loaf bread, and iced tea.

THE PLACE:

        A sign on Hwy. 301 leads motorists to the Duke's location on Whitman St. A clapboard building houses the barbecue buffet of owners, Antley, Meyers, and Kitrell. Long tables and clean floors lead to the rear of the building where the buffet is set up. Seating is provided for 75-80 people, and employees keep close watch over their buffet spread, making certain serving pans are filled to the brim with hot food.

* * * * * * *

BROWN DERBY BAR-B-Q

LOCATION: 1397 Belleville Rd., just off Hwy. 21 in Orangeburg 534-2998

HOURS: Sun.-Thurs. 9 a.m. - 10 p.m. and Fri.-Sat. 9 a.m. - 12 p.m.

TYPE: Regular menu and take-out

PRICES: Dinners-average to high; bulk rates-average

COOKING TECHNIQUE: Open pit - oak

THE BARBECUE:

        Adam Brown has been cooking his barbecue in the same location for 9 years and has 20 years of experience as a pork specialist. Brown's daughter, Essie Fields, said there was "very little" her father didn't know about cooking pork, and the Brown Derby's barbecue bears up to that claim. Brown cooks over oak coals as often as three times a week to meet the demand for his product. The meat is cooked for 8 to 8-1/2 hours and is turned once (after 7 hours) to ensure thorough cooking. Brown subscribes to the cooking theory that a primary sauce must be added late in the cooking process to bring out the real barbecue taste. His product is chopped, then served with a mustard-based sauce that lends a spicy, well-seasoned taste to the meat. Ribs are cooked more than 6 hours, basted, then served with generous meaty portions falling off the bone. Brown's pork ribs were the outstanding item on his barbecue menu, which includes oven-cooked chicken basted with Brown's special sauce. The spicy mixture, put in pint containers, is often sold to Brown's loyal customers. The Brown Derby's menu is well rounded, offering patrons cole slaw, green beans, rice and hash, and macaroni and cheese. Brown believes that open pit cooking is the only way to prepare barbecue.

THE PLACE:

Food orders are given to the kitchen staff through a cubbyhole located behind a bright formica-topped counter at the rear of the dining room. In a matter of minutes, plates bearing generous portions of Brown's special barbecue are being handed to the waitresses through the same slot. The restaurant seats approximately 60 people, and Essie Fields heads a staff of friendly, good-natured employees, who are ready to fill your plates with their highly respected pork-pourri.

* * * * * * *

EARL DUKE'S BAR-B-Q

LOCATION:	North Main St., Cameron 823-2286
HOURS:	Thurs.-Sat. 11 a.m. - 9 p.m.
TYPE:	Buffet, take-out and catering.
PRICES:	Buffet-average; bulk rates-average
COOKING TECHNIQUE:	Electric

THE BARBECUE:

Earl Duke's place in Cameron has one of the grandest reputations ever enjoyed by a barbecue house in South Carolina. After over 24 years in the business, Earl Duke has established one that requires the preparation of over 1,000 pounds of pork every week. The double nuance of nobility in his name is appropriate, since Duke's following is loyal and his barbecue is much-heralded.

Only last year Duke's switched to electric cookers. The hams and shoulders manager Dale Jackson selects for cooking are not smoked, as it is the contention of the Duke's owners that technique, not smoke, is the key to true barbecue taste. The folks who manage the establishment for the now-retired barbecue baron are loyal to Earl Duke's cooking ideology. The pork is prepared in two electric pits by cooking the meat for a full nine hours. A vinegar sauce is added to the pork after five hours, and that sauce is said (by Duke) to be the key to the barbecue taste. Duke's uses a ketchup/mustard mixture for their sauce whose recipe has been handed down to Jackson from Earl Duke himself.

This ensures that Duke's customers are getting the same barbecue Earl Duke was serving for so many years.

Both the chopped barbecue and the ribs served by Duke's were outstanding examples of electric pit excellence. The lightly sauced, chopped pork was succulent to the taste. Ribs were short on meat, but long on flavor, and the pork hash served as a companion dish on the all-you-can-eat buffet was one of the better recipes in this region. The people at Duke's work hard to prove that you don't need an open pit to produce a good barbecue. The buffet is rounded out with two types of pork skins, slaw, pickles (dill and sweet), and loaf bread. The name may be Earl Duke, but he's the King of barbecue in the Cameron area.

THE PLACE:

Earl Duke's is located in a block of old buildings on Main Street, and it may well be the main attraction in Cameron, South Carolina. Upon entering the glass fronted building the customer notices the seemingly endless lines of long metal tables (a typical school cafeteria set-up) and folding chairs sitting on a plain concrete floor. At the rear of the front dining room is a simple stainless steel buffet. To the right, separated by a tall room divider, is an open dining room -- a larger version of the front room. Duke's dining room can seat up to 150 hungry customers.

* * * * * * *

LAIRD'S BAR-B-Q

LOCATION: 1/2 mile south of Hwy. 178 on Hwy. 321
              in North   247-5121

HOURS: Fri. and Sat. 11 a.m. - 9 p.m.

TYPE: Buffet and take-out

PRICES: Buffet-low; dinners-low; bulk rates-average

COOKING
TECHNIQUE: Combination gas/charcoal pit

THE BARBECUE:

Robert Laird has heard about Earl Duke's being the King of Barbecue in the Orangeburg area, but he steadfastly refuses to believe it. The genial owner of Laird's Bar-B-Q has been (without staging any coup)

-53-

moving toward that territorial throne for several years. While he has been cooking barbecue since childhood, Laird has been running a successful barbecue business since 1971. This year he began serving the chopped meat from his gas/charcoal-cooked hams and shoulders in a brand-new facility that stands as testimony to his abilities as a barbecue-preneur. Pork is cooked on pits of Laird's own design for as many as 12 hours. Halfway through the cooking process, the meat is turned to ensure a "deep-cooked" taste. The meat is then chopped and bathed in a vinegar sauce that, when applied to hot pork, "seasons your barbecue".

   The barbecue that reached the buffet line at Laird's was a moist, quite lean, mouth-watering treat for customers. The tomato-based table sauce, a Laird original that he sells by the pint, is, in the owner's words, "milder than the sauce we served in the old days. People can't take the old stuff anymore." His current sauce adds bite to the pork, without overpowering the rich taste of the meat. A mustard-based sauce is used to baste Laird's version of barbecued chicken. While the taste of the chicken suffered from too much tartness due to the sauce, the pieces were tender, meaty, and moist. Laird's hash is a beef/pork (1/3 to 2/3 ratio) mixture that ranks among the best. The all-you-can-eat buffet includes fried chicken, candied yams, loaf bread, and hush puppies. The dessert of the house is red velvet cake, and Laird's homemade pies are local favorites. Robert Laird believes in barbecue as a sound business venture but stresses quality in everything he serves. "A business like this requires a lot of organization. You can't survive without a production line approach. The labor and overhead would just eat you up."

THE PLACE:

   Robert Laird sunk a lot of barbecue bucks into a new building this year. The smell of fresh-cut wood accents that newness in the attractive dining room that features a dark wood decor, soft fluorescent lighting, and comfortable booths that will seat up to 200 patrons. Laird's careful selection of decor has preserved the traditional barbecue atmosphere and allows customers a comfortable dining experience. Laird himself was responsible for the design and construction of this rambling, easily accessible barbecue place.

* * * * * * *

ROGERS BAR-B-QUE

LOCATION: Hwy. 170 (Beaufort Hwy.) about 8 miles east of Hardeeville

HOURS: Uncertain. Rogers was closed by 6 p.m. the Friday I visited the place.

TYPE: Regular menu and take-out

PRICES: Dinners-average; bulk rates-average

COOKING
TECHNIQUE: Uncertain

THE BARBECUE:

    Rogers serves chopped pork, barbecue dinners, and sandwiches of various kinds.

THE PLACE:

    Rogers is located in a white, two-story building that bears a resemblance to many of the country stores in this region of the state. Situated next to Carpenter's Shell Station, the restaurant appeared to have a dining area that could seat about 20 people. Table and counter seating is available.

****

NORTHEAST REGION

****

MOREE'S BAR-B-Q

LOCATION: Near Andrews - 1.7 miles off Hwy. 41 on Hwy. 527   221-5643

HOURS: Fri. and Sat. 5 p.m. - 10 p.m. Usually closed the first two weeks in July.

TYPE: Buffet, take-out, and catering

PRICES: Buffet-average; dinners-average; bulk rates-average

COOKING TECHNIQUE: Open pit - oak (charcoal, too, if necessary)

THE BARBECUE:

     The Bob Moree family handles their barbecue enterprise multi-handedly on all levels. They grow the corn that feeds the hogs that they raise to make the barbecue. They have been operating this way for 12 years. The hogs are put on the open oak pit Wednesday at 2 a.m. and the next morning they are turned and seasoned. The variety of the barbecue the Morees serve is unmatched. They offer two kinds of chopped pork barbecue: one with a medium-hot vinegar-based sauce and the other with a hot sauce blended in. The only difference between the two is the degree of hotness of the sauces, so customers can let their taste buds direct them to whichever type they prefer. The meat in both was lean, chunky, and full of delicious smoked flavor. The juicy chicken meat was so tender that it was literally falling off the bone. A rich tomato sauce covered the chicken -- as well as the long juicy ribs. The Morees offer two types of skins, too. One kind is fried to a light, airy crispness, and the other is the skin taken directly from the cooked hog. The consistency and texture were quite different from any skin I have ever tasted. It was thick and leathery, but the sour vinegar taste was good. Along with these items on the all-you-can-eat buffet are rice and gravy (a thin mixture made with all the remaining parts of the cooked hogs), two types of pork hash (medium and hot -- both quite savory), sweet potatoes, bread and butter pickles, cole slaw, loaf bread, chocolate cake, coconut cake, and tea and coffee. Everything except the bread is homemade. The Morees love seeing their customers enjoy the barbecue and specialities so much that they often encourage diners to help themselves to seconds.

THE PLACE:

This low cement-block building is easy to pass by, and a faded "Moree's Bar-B-Q" sign is barely detectable unless you are looking closely for it. To the left of the entrance is a take-out window that offers quick service for carry-out plates, sandwiches, and bulk orders. Two long tables with wooden chairs are in each of the two dining rooms, which seat 40 and 75. Do not be discouraged by the "Club Members Only" sign on the front door. Walk on in and dig in to some of the best barbecue in South Carolina.

* * * * * * *

TISDALE'S BAR-B-Q

LOCATION: Take Hwy. 527 from Kingstree to the third paved road on the left beyond the city limits (about 6 miles). A partially obscured sign will indicate where to turn. A 2 mile drive down this road leads to the second Tisdale's sign, indicating a right turn into the Cedar Swamp region. Tisdale's is on the right. 382-2799

HOURS: Tisdale's is open only on Fridays from 6 p.m. until the customers quit coming. Closed between May and September.

TYPE: Buffet, take-out and catering

PRICES: Buffet-high; bulk rates-high

COOKING
TECHNIQUE: Open pit - oak

THE BARBECUE:

It takes a barbecue fanatic to brave the wilds of the country around Kingstree in search of Tisdale's barbecue. Pork lovers should travel with a friend whose sole purpose during the fifteen minute drive beyond the city limits is to watch for the aged signs that indicate the turning points. Donald and Elise Tisdale have been cooking their barbecue out in the Cedar Swamp area for "too many years to count", according to Donald, and folks travel a long way to get a taste of the pit-cooked pork. Donald Tisdale cooks whole hogs more than 12 hours to ensure a well-cooked barbecue. The oak-smoked meat is thoroughly sauced with a vinegar/pepper mixture during the cooking process. This same sauce is Tisdale's table sauce. He believes in enhancing the taste of the meat -- not covering it with ketchup/mustard sauces. The Tisdales' all-you-can-eat buffet offers customers hand-shredded pork barbecue, pork hash, gravy, yams, cole slaw, pickles, loaf bread, and Elise Tisdale's homemade cake. Tisdale's is a family-run operation, and love of cooking -- not money -- keeps the pit barbecue coming back every fall.

THE PLACE:

      Tisdale's roomy, white building is located in a neatly mowed field next to their home in Cedar Swamp. Donald Tisdale furnished his barbecue house with hand-built tables and chairs. Over 80 customers can sit in the dining room and help themselves to a barbecue feast a la Donald and Elise Tisdale.

                  * * * * * * *

COUNTRY COUSIN BAR-B-QUE

LOCATION: Hwy. 52 South, Scranton 389-4545

HOURS: Thurs.-Sat. 11 a.m. - 10 p.m.

TYPE: Buffet, take-out and catering

PRICES: Buffet-average; bulk rates-average

COOKING
TECHNIQUE: Combination gas/charcoal pit

THE BARBECUE:

      Carol Haseldon and Dot Kirby, two of the friendliest people we've talked with in the barbecue business, have operated Country Cousin for 9 years. Using two large gas and charcoal pits, they cook the entire hog for 8-9 hours, saucing throughout the process. For their weekend crowds, the owners cook over 4,000 pounds of barbecue. One word can describe their barbecue sauce: HOT! All types of meat served-chopped and chunked, pork, ribs, and chicken are well flavored with a hot sauce of vinegar, pepper, and tomato. The chopped pork was lean, moist, and flavorful. The ribs, heavily basted with the same peppery sauce, were not very meaty, but they were good and chewy. Generously coated with a rich tomato sauce, the chicken was tender and peppery. Served with the buffet were pork skins (light and crisp), liver hash, chicken bog (as peppery as the barbecue chicken), yams, slaw, pickles, loaf bread and tea.

THE PLACE:

    The sprawling, yellow cement-block building is not easy to miss. Inside is one large dining room that can be divided into smaller sections by accordion screens. Green cement-block and wood-paneled walls have few decorations. Designed for families and large groups, Country Cousin is furnished with long tables and wooden ladder-back chairs, seating 115.

* * * * * * *

FRED GASKINS' GROCERY

LOCATION: Off Hwy. 378 on Hwy. 341, 4 miles east of Lake City   389-1440

HOURS: Mon.-Sat. 7:30 a.m. - 7:30 p.m.

TYPE: Take-out only

PRICES: Bulk rates-average

COOKING
TECHNIQUE: Gas

THE BARBECUE:

    When Fred Gaskins opened his grocery store he used charcoal, but now he has switched to gas to cook the shoulders and loins for his barbecue. Gaskins' wholesale barbecue business has been going strong for many years. The chopped barbecued pork was moist and mushy, with a distinct vinegar flavor. The sauce that he makes and sells by the pint is composed mainly of vinegar, ketchup, and red and black pepper. Barbecue may be bought by the pound or by the sandwich.

THE PLACE:

    This white service station/grocery store stands between a fork in the highway, so it's not easy to miss. A faded sign, however, is the only indication that barbecue is sold there. Inside is a variety of goods for sale -- from hardware and household staples to insect repellent and fishing tackle. Wedged in a back corner of the tiny, cluttered country store is a well-packed meat counter and a miniscule kitchen area where Gaskins prepares barbecue sandwiches and weighs meat for the customers.

* * * * * * *

OWEN'S BAR-B-Q

LOCATION: Hwy. 378, 1 mile east of Lake City 394-2378

HOURS: Mon.-Sat. 8 a.m. - 8 p.m.

TYPE: Regular menu and take-out

PRICES: Dinners-average; bulk rates-average

COOKING
TECHNIQUE: Open pit - coke briquets

THE BARBECUE:

Owen's Bar-B-Q, now owned and operated by Chessie Owens, was established in 1946 by her late husband Mellon. The barbecue is still prepared the way Mr. Owens always prepared it. After the Boston butts have cooked all night over charcoal, they are chopped and sauced with a hot, spicy mixture of pepper, mustard, vinegar and tomato. The resulting barbecue was almost too moist with a strong spicy-hot flavor. Sliced barbecue (thicker portions of the same stuff) and barbecued chicken are also served. The hot sauce, a popular item among the clientele at Owen's, is bottled and sold by the pint. Other food offered includes chicken and rice, chicken and dumplings, country-styled steak, and fresh vegetables.

THE PLACE:

This tiny white building contains a room that looks as if nothing has changed since 1946. In it are worn booths, scarred metal kitchen tables and chairs, a long counter and a few stools, with seating for fifty. A faded exterior sign is easy to miss, so the customer must watch closely.

* * * * * * *

CAIN'S BAR-B-Q

LOCATION: Hwy. 51 (Pamplico Hwy.), just outside the business district of Florence, 2 miles southeast of Coles Crossroads 662-8991

HOURS: Thurs.-Sat. 11 a.m. - 10 p.m.

TYPE: Regular menu, take-out and catering

PRICES: Dinners-average; bulk rates-average

COOKING
TECHNIQUE: Electric

THE BARBECUE:

    Cain's Bar-B-Q has an interesting history behind its development. Thirty years ago, Woodrow W. and Nita Moore Cain from Pamplico, South Carolina, opened a country store with an adjacent dining room. They kept a mailing list of customers and when they planned to cook barbecue (about every two weeks), they sent out notices to those on the list. In 1965 they built across the street from their original location and have been operating this establishment ever since. Some changes have been made. Woodrow Cain does not have to rely on a mailing list anymore, and he has modernized his cooking technique. Still using whole hogs, he now has four large electric pits (each can hold about three hogs) that do the cooking much more quickly and efficiently than the original hickory/oak pit. The process takes three people about eight hours. First, the heads and feet are removed; then the hogs are cooked without seasoning or turning for eight hours. Next, the meat is stripped from the bone, chopped, sauced and mixed thoroughly. It is then ready to be served in sandwiches and on plate dinners.

    The barbecued pork, finely minced, was complimented by sweet sauce that had a slightly hot, lingering flavor. The minced barbecue's taste was pleasant. Juicy and tender, the chicken was coated with a thick tomato sauce which was delicious enough to eat by itself. It's Nita Cain's own recipe, and she encourages her customers to ask for extra amounts to dip the chicken in. One of the items most in demand at Cain's is the chicken bog, a moist, mildly seasoned dish of chunky chicken and rice -- heavier on the chicken than the rice. Almost as popular seems to be the liver hash, and another specialty, rice with red gravy, was sweet and tangy. Accompanying the barbecue are yams, cole slaw, hush puppies (Nita Cain suggested we try them dipped in her BBQ sauce for chicken), and sweet pickles. Cain's barbecue fans can also find it served at Southside Pharmacy, 6th Avenue, Myrtle Beach.

THE PLACE:

Cain's Bar-B-Q has a cafeteria feel to the place. Customers are seated at simple-looking tables and served bountiful plates of Cain's pork amidst fresh scrubbed surroundings. The kitchen area of the restaurant runs alongside the main dining area - a narrow, plain room that runs deep toward the rear of the building. A second dining area is available for the larger crowds that flock to Cain's during the busy weekend hours.

* * * * * * *

WOODY'S BARBECUE

LOCATION: Hwy. 51 (Pamplico Hwy.) just outside the business district of Florence 662-3347 or 493-5438

HOURS: Thurs.-Sat. 11 a.m. - 10 p.m.

TYPE: Regular menu, take-out and catering

PRICES: Dinners-low to average; bulk rates-average

COOKING TECHNIQUE: Gas

THE BARBECUE:

J.W. Hyman began experimenting with cooking barbecue on the open pit using oak and hickory years ago. In 1956 this restaurant was opened. Hyman uses a sheltered open gas pit to barbecue his locally-bought hogs. During the first 4-1/2 hours, the hogs are cooked meat side down. Then they are turned and a seasoning sauce applied. For another 2-1/2 hours the pork is cooked; afterwards, it is chopped and basted again with another sauce. Hyman has set up his gas pit to cook 3, 5, 7 or 10 hogs at a time, averaging 350 pounds of meat per cooking. The barbecue was cut into moist, lean chunks. Although not on the menu, pork ribs can be had for the asking. What little meat there was on them was extremely greasy. Very proud of his special sauce that goes into the barbecue, Mr. Hyman remarked, "My wife doesn't even know my sauce recipe." In addition to the chopped pork barbecue and ribs, Woody's serves barbecued chicken, chicken bog, liver hash, quail, hot dogs and spahetti. Homemade hushpuppies, slaw (made with sweet red relish and pickles) and sweet pickles are staple barbecue accompaniments.

THE PLACE:

Walking into Woody's Barbecue is like walking into one of the diner scenes from a Humphrey Bogart movie - lots of dark wood and plain wooden tables. Woody's can seat up to 150 people in the main dining area, and Hyman keeps what he referred to as a "nicer" dining room for private parties.

* * * * * * *

BOB'S BAR-B-Q

LOCATION: 2131 Hofmeyer Rd. (behind Shoney's), Florence 669-8644

HOURS: Mon.-Sat. 11 a.m. - 9 p.m.

TYPE: Regular menu and take-out

PRICES: Dinners-average; bulk rates-average

COOKING
TECHNIQUE: Electric

THE BARBECUE:

For seven years Bob Hyman has operated his barbecue establishment, cooking whole pigs on large electric pits. Extra seasoning is applied after the hogs have cooked 8-10 hours. Although lean and moist, the chopped barbecue was somewhat bland tasting. Customers may spice up their pork with Coleman's BBQ Sauce, a 40-50 year-old recipe of vinegar, mustard, pepper, and other ingredients. This commercially sold sauce (bottled in Florence) had a rather hot aftertaste. A popular item in this section of the state, chicken bog, tasted more of rice than chicken. Accompanying the barbecue dinners are homemade hush puppies and cole slaw. A full menu, from seafood and steaks to liver hash and fried chicken, is available.

THE PLACE:

Two simply decorated, wood-paneled dining rooms seat about 100 customers.

* * * * * * *

DANIEL'S AND RAY'S BARBECUE

LOCATION: Hwy. 76, near the Hwy. 9 junction in Nichols   526-2419

HOURS: Mon.-Thurs. 11 a.m. - 3 p.m. and Fri.-Sat. 11 a.m. - 9 p.m.

TYPE: Buffet and take-out

PRICES: Buffet-average; dinners-average; bulk rates-average

COOKING TECHNIQUE: Open pit - wood

THE BARBECUE:

Howard and Judy Ray bought this established business from the Daniel family this year, and with the restaurant came the tried-and-true recipes of the Daniels. The chopped barbecue served at the Rays' all-you-can-eat buffet table was lean, moist, and chunky. Select shoulders are cooked over wood for more than twelve hours to guarantee a rich smoked taste. The meat was tender but left a spicy aftertaste, probably due to the Rays' sauce, which was very tart and spicy. The buffet also features chicken bog (an unusual dish found also in the Florence area), rice and gravy, fried chicken, barbecued beans, cole slaw, and yams.

THE PLACE:

Brown, ranch-style construction marks the home of the Rays' barbecue. The trim-looking building is located at the rear of a large gravel parking lot on Hwy. 76. A walk-up, carry-out window is provided for travelers who want to pick up a quick snack. Inside, the restaurant is outfitted in a yellow and brown color scheme. Brown tiled floors, large latticed windows, and bright fluorescent lighting are the eye-openers in the barbecue house. Over 80 people can sit at restaurant-style tables and chairs and enjoy pit-cooked pork and trimmings.

* * * * * * *

PINETUCKET BAR-B-Q BARN

LOCATION: Hwy. 501, 2 miles from Aynor 358-8222

HOURS: Mon.-Sat. 11 a.m. - 9 p.m.

TYPE: Buffet and take-out

PRICES: Buffet-average; bulk rates-average

COOKING
TECHNIQUE: Electric

THE BARBECUE:

      The owner, Mrs. Skipper, refused to answer most of my questions. So, here's all I have gleaned from my visit at Pinetucket. The barbecue establishment opened December 7, 1978, and the pork is cooked on electric pits. The buffet (all-you-can-eat) features chopped barbecue, barbecued chicken, pork skins, pork sausage (an unusual addition to the fare), liver hash and rice, candied yams, green beans, slaw, pickles and corn muffins. A thin vinegar-based sauce accompanies the barbecued pork.

THE PLACE:

      Two small dining rooms, simply but nicely decorated and furnished with tables for 4, 6, 8 or more, can accommodate about 50 people. Adjacent to the Bar-B-Q Barn is Pinetucket Meats, a large, brightly-lit meat market that sells all types of pork and beef -- from pigs' feet and knuckles to sirloin steaks and ham hocks.

* * * * * * *

RADD DEW'S BAR-B-Q

LOCATION: Hwy. 701, 2 miles south of Conway 397-3453

HOURS: Fri. and Sat. 5 p.m. - 9 p.m.

TYPE: Buffet, take-out and catering

PRICES: Buffet-average; bulk rates-low

COOKING
TECHNIQUE: Two different techniques: one - open pit-black jack oak and hickory; the other - electric

THE BARBECUE:

Known by many as the "Bar-B-Q King of Horry County", Radd Dew began selling barbecue in 1956 in plastic bags because he couldn't find tubs large enough. Today his wholesale business in both North and South Carolina is booming, and he now sells two kinds of barbecue, one that is electrically-cooked (the red label) and one that is wood-cooked (the brown label). His restaurant, which opened in 1970, serves the original hickory and oak-cooked barbecue, made from Boston butts. On the all-you-can-eat buffet is lean, chopped barbecue that had a strong smoked flavor and a slight vinegar taste. The sauce recipe, over a century old, has a vinegar/spice base. With the buffet are rice and hash (made of pork and liver), french fries, string beans, candied yams, hush puppies, rolls, cole slaw, apple sauce, pickles and iced tea. In years past, Radd Dew has supplied drug and grocery stores throughout the state with his brands of barbecue. Today, Radd Dew's barbecue and sauce are sold in many of the Conway and Myrtle Beach area restaurants.

THE PLACE:

Situated beside his own home, Radd Dew's Bar-B-Q is a simple wooden building with a wood-shingled roof. The pleasant furnishings consist of formica-topped wooden tables, plain wooden chairs, and a tiled floor. The small restaurant's atmosphere is friendly and inviting. Seating capcity is 60.

* * * * * * *

THE RED BARN BAR-B-Q

LOCATION: Windy Hill Shopping Center, Hwy. 17 -
                 Windy Hill Beach   272-6932

HOURS: Mon. 11 a.m. - 9 p.m. and Tues.-Sat.
                 11 a.m. - 10 p.m. during the summer.
                 Winter hours may vary

TYPE: Regular menu and take-out

PRICES: Dinners-high; bulk rates-high

COOKING
TECHNIQUE: Electric cooker - hickory-smoked

THE BARBECUE:

      Opened in 1976, The Red Barn has always offered a variety of barbecue. Owner Len Bottomley electrically cooks shoulders and Boston butts for the chopped pork barbecue, back beef ribs, barbecued beef and barbecued chicken. The chopped pork was somewhat fatty and the beef ribs were spare on meat. Two sauces, a hot and a mild, are offered. Even though The Red Barn advertises that their barbecue is hickory-smoked, there was no detectable smoked flavor in any of the meat tasted. All barbecue plates are accompanied by giblet gravy and rice, hash (made with ground beef) and rice, or french fries; candied yams; cole slaw; and homemade hush puppies (heavy but tasty). Also on the menu are Brunswick stew, barbecued beans, barbecue slaw (with a red tinge, a crunchy texture, and a barbecued flavor) and various sandwiches.

THE PLACE:

      The exterior of this tiny restaurant resembles its name. After the customer orders at a small window and receives his food, he sits at one of the tables covered with red and white checked oil cloth. The floors, walls and chairs are all wooden, and displayed farm tools and a stuffed boar's head contribute to the barn atmosphere. The Red Barn seats 50 people.

* * * * * * *

BIG D'S BAR-B-Q I

LOCATION: Hwy. 41, about halfway between Johnsonville
            and Hemingway   558-2661

HOURS: Fri. and Sat. 10 a.m. - 9:30 p.m.

TYPE: Buffet, take-out and catering

PRICES: Buffet-average; bulk rates-average

COOKING
TECHNIQUE: Electric

THE BARBECUE:

      Davol Davis began his barbecue restaurant almost nine years ago, and for the first three he cooked only with wood. Now he has switched to using electric pits to cook the whole hogs. During the 8-9 hour cooking process, he occasionally sauces the hogs. His sauce recipe, at least 60 years old, has vinegar as its base. It was thin but quite tangy. A different sauce (that appears to be more tomatoey) covers the chicken. The chopped barbecue was lean and moist with a light sauce flavor. The ribs were spare on meat and flavor. Also served on the buffet were skins (light and crisp), yams, liver, gravy and rice, and slaw.

THE PLACE:

      This large open building has a "barn" decor with wagon wheel lighting fixtures, displays of farm tools, and oil cloth-covered tables for large groups. The dining room (seating 100) has an atmosphere not unlike some of the family steak houses.

* * * * * * *

BIG D'S BAR-B-Q II

LOCATION: Hwy. 17, Surfside Beach (across from Ocean
                  Lakes Family Campground) 238-5818

HOURS: April-December, Tues.-Sat. 11 a.m. - 10 p.m.
                  Winter hours vary

TYPE: Buffet, take-out and catering

PRICES: Buffet-high; bulk rates-average

COOKING
TECHNIQUE: Electric

THE BARBECUE:

  John Van Davis, brother of Davol Davis who owns Big D's in Hemingway, has operated this restaurant for seven years. The cooking process, the type barbecue, and the sauce are the same as his brother's. See "Big D's I" entry for Hemingway for more details. The only difference in the buffet is that the Surfside establishment also serves homemade sweet potato pudding (an unusual item for a South Carolina barbecue buffet), giblet gravy and cornbread. Surfside's buffet price is also a little higher. Both Big D's serve a typical barbecue fare.

THE PLACE:

  The restaurant, seating 140, is a larger version of the Hemingway location.

****

SOUTH CENTRAL REGION

****

THE 'QUE-PIT

LOCATION: Hwy. 76 By-Pass, near downtown Newberry
276-9950

HOURS: Thurs.-Sat. 11 a.m. - 9 p.m.

TYPE: Buffet and take-out

PRICES: Buffet-average; bulk rates-average

COOKING
TECHNIQUE: Charcoal briquets and hickory

THE BARBECUE:

    The 'Que-Pit, opened in April 1979, is owned and run by Howard Smith and Frank Courtney, who have been cooking barbecue almost all their lives. Their all-you-can-eat buffet features the usual minced pork barbecue, pork hash, pork ribs, and barbecued chicken, but Smith and Courtney have added several other specialites: barbecued rabbit and beef ribs. The minced barbecue is made from hams and shoulders that have cooked about 6-8 hours over charcoal briquets and hickory. The owners sauce all meat (except for the hams and shoulders that will make the minced) on the pit, after it is about 90% cooked. A mustard sauce, whose recipe is over 10 years old, is the base for all the meat except ribs. The sauce is kept simmering in a pot on the buffet line. The minced pork was lean and succulent, and the mustard-based sauce brought out the pork flavor. The pork ribs were not as meaty as the beef ribs, which had a delicious tomato and spice taste. The barbecued rabbit had a smoked taste similar to, but sweeter than, the chicken. Howard Smith highly recommended the rabbit (which we have not found in any other South Carolina barbecue house) because it contains "less cholesterol and more protein ounce for ounce than all other meat." The 'Que-Pit's buffet also includes barbecued beans, slaw, corn on the cob and other vegetables.

THE PLACE:

This new restaurant building, which seats 116, is simply and tastefully furnished with tables, chairs and a few frills. It's designed for people more interested in food than atmosphere.

* * * * * * *

WISE'S BAR-B-Q

LOCATION: Hwy. 76, 8 miles from Newberry towards Clinton 276-6699 or 276-4461

HOURS: Fri.-Sat. 8 a.m. - 10 p.m.

TYPE: Buffet and take-out

PRICES: Buffet-average; bulk rates-average

COOKING
TECHNIQUE: Gas

THE BARBECUE:

James E. and John W. Wise have operated Wise's Bar-B-Q for 9 years. On two large gas pits, the Wise brothers cook about 2,000 pounds of barbecue and 100 gallons of hash a week. For the chopped barbecue they cook pork hams about 16-20 hours, turning and seasoning them often. The meat served on the Wise's buffet (all-you-can-eat) is chopped pork, barbecued chicken, barbecued ribs, and hash. One sauce (with a strong mustard, vinegar, and black pepper taste) is served with the barbecue and may be purchased by the pint. The chopped pork was lean, moist, and flavorful, but had no smoked taste. The chicken had only a slight barbecue flavor, and the hash, composed of pork and beef, was well-seasoned with plenty of pepper. Included in the buffet are sweet and sour pickles, cole slaw, white loaf bread and iced tea.

THE PLACE:

Wise's low white cement block restaurant is easy to pass if you're not looking closely. Inside the drab building are long metal tables and folding chairs that seat 80. The windowless walls lack adornment. Filled tea pitchers are on every table.

* * * * * * *

STOCKMAN'S BAR-B-Q PLACE

LOCATION: Amick's Ferry Road, 5 or 6 miles from Prosperity 364-2884

HOURS: Hours vary from season to season, but generally every other Sat. all day (until sold out)

TYPE: Take-out only

PRICES: Bulk rates-average

COOKING
TECHNIQUE: Open pit over hickory

THE BARBECUE:

      The Robert Stockman family has been cooking barbecue fifteen years. They spend the entire day before they open preparing the pits, burning the wood to get it ready for cooking, and barbecuing the whole hogs (about 12 hours). They sell their barbecue (hams, loins, ribs) only by the pound. Their special homemade sauce has mustard base. Unfortunately, the day I visited the Stockman's, they were cooking the hogs. Because the meat was not ready, I was not able to sample it.

THE PLACE:

      Stockman's Bar-B-Q Place is easy to miss. The pink cement block building has a faded, obscure sign out front. Behind this building is a large screened room containing three large pits and stacks of hickory limbs and branches. Inside is one simple room -- no sit-down area for eating -- containing scales for weighing the meat and a long counter for wrapping it and serving the customers.

* * * * * * *

FULMER'S BAR-B-Q

LOCATION: Hwy. 1, less than a mile south of the
            I-26 interchange, Aiken 648-1093

HOURS: Presently closed. Will open in the fall
            of 1979 in a new facility at the same
            location.

* * * * * * *

CROSBY'S BAR-B-Q

LOCATION: Hwy. 19, 8 miles south of Aiken (approxi-
            mately 3 miles north of New Ellenton)
            649-4260

HOURS: Tues.-Sat. 10 a.m. - 9 p.m. and Sun.
            10 a.m. - 3 p.m.

TYPE: Buffet, take-out and catering

PRICES: Buffet-average; bulk rates-average

COOKING
TECHNIQUE: Electric cookers

THE BARBECUE:

    Charles Crosby has been cooking pork hams in the same location for about 25 years and is the recognized local authority on barbecue. Years of cooking have resulted in a consistently good barbecue. The addition of Crosby's spicy-hot ketchup/mustard sauce disguised any flavor distinctions. The table sauce is the ketchup/mustard mixture that Crosby applies to the pork after cooking. Crosby's sliced pork differed only in texture, not taste. Crosby rounds out his buffet with tender, juicy chicken (barbecued with the same sauce), cole slaw, all-pork hash and rice, potato salad, vegetables, loaf bread, and hush puppies (light and crispy).

THE PLACE:

A sprawling, beige building perched on the front of a grassy open field is the home of Crosby's barbecue. The two dining rooms at Crosby's are wood-paneled, and metal-legged kitchen tables provide seating for around 100 customers. A large brick, open-faced oven located on the wall behind the buffet serving area adds a touch of old-times to the otherwise commonplace dining area.

* * * * * * *

CAROLINA BAR-B-Q

LOCATION:	109 Main St. (Hwy. 19), New Ellenton 652-9919
HOURS:	Thurs.-Sat. 10 a.m. - 9 p.m.
TYPE:	Buffet and take-out
PRICES:	Buffet-average; dinners-average; bulk rates-low (but Walker is planning an increase in prices).
COOKING TECHNIQUE:	Open pit-charcoal

THE BARBECUE:

Jess Walker, Jr.; his mother, Willie Mae; and brother-in-law, Don Harrison, share the chores at the Carolina Bar-B-Q in downtown New Ellenton. A family recipe dating back over forty years is used in preparing pork hams and shoulders for the restaurant's hungry customers. Meat remains unturned for over 10 hours on the hot charcoal pit located just behind the restaurant. A mild, ketchup-based primary sauce is used to baste the pork sections as soon as they are removed from the pit racks. The pork is then coarsely chopped and served as part of the buffet offering. The meat was slightly fatty, but a delicious charcoal taste made the excess fat seem relatively unimportant. Though the pork was a little dry when served, the addition of either Walker's mild or medium sauce (made available for customers to purchase) provided moisture and just the right amount of spice to the meat. Only the bravest diners use Walker's hot sauce, which is almost volcanic. Cole slaw, potato salad, BBQ beans, hush puppies (homemade), corn, hash (a pork/potato/onion mixture), pickles and loaf bread are part of the buffet, and customers can enjoy a respectable version of barbecued chicken, if they prefer poultry, at no extra cost.

THE PLACE:

A huge tan and brown paint job on the north side of this red brick building proudly proclaims the two story structure's status as the home of Carolina Bar-B-Q. Wide awnings shade big, open windows at the front of the building, and customers entering the dining area can fill their plates from the shiny buffet at the rear of the open dining room. Folding and picnic-style tables provide the sitting and the setting for Jess Walker's brand of South Carolina pit-cooked barbecue. The restaurant seats approximately 60 people.

* * * * * * *

CHAVOUS PIT COOKED BAR-B-Q

LOCATION: North of the Hwy. 278 and 302 crossroads on Hwy. 278 near Beech Island

HOURS: Mon.-Sat. 10 a.m. - 9 p.m.

TYPE: Regular menu and take-out.

PRICES: Dinners-low

COOKING
TECHNIQUE: Open pit - oak and hickory

THE BARBECUE:

Chavous Pit Cooked Bar-B-Q is more of a "pit stop" than a restaurant. Located adjacent to the Chavous brothers' service garage, the barbecue place is run by Jimmie Chavous as a sideline to the brothers' auto enterprise. Chavous prepares whole hogs on a small brick pit, using the method his father originated. Racks hold the pork only two feet above a thin layer of glowing coals for 8-9 hours. The family's own ketchup-based sauce is applied after the meat is cooked. Chavous serves the juicy pork chopped or sliced to order. The pork had a sooty taste that tended to shroud the meat's natural flavor. Jimmie Chavous's barbecue business is bolstered by sales of cold beer and sandwiches.

THE PLACE:

Located on a lonely stretch of Hwy. 278 between Beech Island and New Ellenton, Chavous Pit Cooked

Bar-B-Q is housed in a white concrete-block building next to a multi-bay garage. Inside, the restaurant/beer joint offers only a few counter seats, making take-out a must. Wood paneling and pool tables complete the decor.

* * * * * * *

SMOKEY PORKERS BAR-B-Q

LOCATION: 1016 Sandbar Ferry Rd. Beech Island 827-1559

HOURS: Mon.-Fri. 11:30 a.m. - 3 p.m.

TYPE: Regular menu and take-out

PRICES: Dinners-average

COOKING
TECHNIQUE: Electric cooker - hickory-smoked

THE BARBECUE:

"My husband was Mr. Barbecue around these parts." Ada Collins is proud of the reputation her late husband owned concerning his pit cooking ability. Gilbert Collins came to the state from Georgia over 40 years ago to establish a barbecue restaurant. Gone is the open pit, Gilbert Collins, and the one hundred-year-old plantation cooking method Collins employed. Ada; her gospel-singing daughter, Flo Carter; and son-in-law, John Ginn, incorporate the old cooking method with electric cooking to produce a respectable pork barbecue. The family uses only hams in the 9 hour preparation of their chopped pork. The barbecue was a bit moist, and ribs at Smokey Porkers were lean, thickly basted and meaty. The chicken was tender, basted with a mild ketchup-based sauce Ada Collins prepares (customers can buy limited quantities for their own consumption) and just as meaty as the ribs. Ada Collins' homemade cornbread alone makes a trip to this restaurant a must. The tall, moist servings of this baked golden grain will virtually melt in your mouth. The taste was more akin to that of cake than to cornmeal. If you still have room for dessert, Ada Collins has just the dish. Her fresh baked pies encourage customers to loosen their belts and forget dieting. If that isn't enough, side orders of macaroni and cheese and potato salad provide space fillers on the heaping plates of food served here.

THE PLACE:

      Smokey Porkers looks like a restaurant fallen on hard times. All around the dining room are the lackluster signs of an aging enterprise. Still, the owners have managed a "kitchen table" atmosphere in their little restaurant. The color scheme in the building is as yellow as Ada's flakey cornbread and the Collins/Carter friendliness is an ever-present fixture.

* * * * * * *

FREEMAN'S BBQ

LOCATION:	1008 Sandbar Ferry Rd. (Hwy. 78), Beech Island
HOURS:	Thurs.-Sat. 7 a.m. - 11 p.m.
TYPE:	Regular menu and take-out
PRICES:	Dinner-average; bulk rates-average to high
COOKING TECHNIQUE:	Open pit - charcoal and hickory

THE BARBECUE:

      James Freeman has been cooking barbecue in the Beech Island area for over thirty years. He handles all the cooking chores around the smoky open pit, while other family members greet customers and serve heaping portions of well-cooked pork. Freeman's barbecue is true to the traditional techniques and taste. He cooks whole hogs up to 8 hours, turning the meat only once to ensure thorough, even cooking. Freeman makes use of the best cuts of pork in his chopped barbecue, fries the pork skins to a delicate crispness, and uses other lean pork portions in the making of his pork hash. He makes the pork ribs available to his customers while the supply lasts. The chipped and sliced pork is sauced with a vinegar sauce after cooking, and two varieties of table sauce are made available to patrons. The barbecue was moist, juicy, slightly seasoned, and very well smoked in its taste. Ribs were meaty and moist, and Freeman's brand of pork skins had an indescribably good taste. The addition of mild table sauce made for a mouth-watering barbecue dinner. Hot sauce is for the braver patrons who don't mind tear-streaked cheeks. Finally, Freeman's barbecued chicken was meaty, though somewhat dry, and was best with the addition of extra sauce. Barbecue is Freeman's specialty and he refuses to burden his menu with additional items.

THE PLACE:

      Freeman's is designed for take-out eating. A dilapidated shack houses the pit area and the few tables and counter seats that make up the dining area, but don't let the looks of the building keep you from trying this top notch barbecue. It's common knowledge among barbecue connoisseurs that the best pork is seldom found in the most sparkling surroundings. Freeman seems content to keep his pit area clean and his clientele moving.

                    * * * * * * *

EDMUNDS BAR-B-QUE

LOCATION:	511 Edgefield Rd. (Hwy.25) 2 miles south of the I-20 interchange in N. Augusta. You'll recognize the building by the giant "E" on the red brick chimney
HOURS:	Tues.-Sat. 10 a.m. - 8 p.m.
TYPE:	Regular menu, take-out and catering
PRICES:	Dinner-average; bulk rates-average
COOKING TECHNIQUE:	Electric cooker - hickory-smoked

THE BARBECUE:

      Cleve Edmunds has been cooking barbecue since 1951. Edmunds' father and father-in-law were barbecuing men in their time, and Cleve has combined the best of both family's recipes to make an electric-cooked pork that is satisfying. Edmunds and his wife Phyllis have operated Edmunds Bar-B-Que since 1969, cooking 2,000 to 2,500 pounds of shoulders every week. They have seved as caterers to P.G.A. officials in nearby Augusta, Georgia, during the Master's tournament and are currently courting New York restauranteurs who plan to turn the operation in the direction of east coast franchising. Edmunds cooks pork shoulders up to 12 hours in electric ovens using hickory chips to give his barbecue a rich, smoked flavor. A mild ketchup-based sauce is applied liberally after the pork is cooked. The resulting barbecue, an above-average brand of electric-cooked pork, was very finely chopped, moist and tender. Chickens are oven baked, then sauced, and hash at Edmunds is an all meat, pork hash that is a cut above the stardard barbecue fare. The

-79-

menu of the restaurant includes chicken stew (unusual for the region), potato salad, cole slaw (tart, mayonnaise variety) and sweet pickles.

THE PLACE:

A simple, low-chimneyed, red brick building is the North Augusta home of Edmunds Bar-B-Que. Inside, picnic tables covered with bright oil cloth provide seating for up to 80 customers. Pork lovers traveling through North Augusta should watch carefully, because the building is set back from the highway just enough to make it difficult to spot. Watch for the squat-looking bait and tackle shop located within 50 yards of Edmunds.

* * * * * * *

EDMUNDS BAR-B-Q

LOCATION: 1307 Richland Ave. (Hwy. 1 and 78), a few blocks from downtown Aiken 649-4044

HOURS: Tues.-Sat. 10 a.m. - 8 p.m.

TYPE: Regular menu, take-out and catering

PRICES: Dinners-average; bulk rate-average

COOKING
TECHNIQUE: Electric-cooked - hickory-smoked

THE BARBECUE:

(See "Edmunds Bar-B-Que" North Augusta entry)

THE PLACE:

A beige, concrete block building provides a home for the second Edmunds location in S.C. Expansive windows make for a brightly lit dining area. Located in a heavy traffic district of Aiken, the trim-looking, low-ceilinged building seats 35 customers.

* * * * * * *

BARBECUE DINER

LOCATION:	Atomic Rd. (Hwy. 125), 3-1/2 miles south of North Augusta
HOURS:	Fri.-Sun. 11 a.m. - 9 p.m.
TYPE:	Regular menu and take-out
PRICES:	Dinners-average
COOKING TECHNIQUE:	Open pit - charcoal

THE BARBECUE:

     Leroy and Carrie Jessie opened this barbecue emporium on the 4th of July in 1979, in time for the holiday rush that is so familiar to barbecue owners. Leroy learned the pit-cooking trade from his father starting out using wood coals, then turning to charcoal as a less expensive and easier managed heat source. The Jessie's cook whole hogs for at least eight hours, turning the meat twice during the cooking process. A salt/vinegar mixture is applied to the meat late in the cooking procedure. This is a cooking extra Leroy Jessie claims brings out the true barbecue taste of the meat. After cooking, the meat is basted with a mustard/ketchup sauce that has just a trace of spice mixed in. Served either chopped or sliced, the pork was tender, moist, and rich in smoked taste. Ribs are available while the supply lasts. The table sauce is the same mixture applied by Jessie following the cooking of the meat. Leroy and Carrie Jessie are newcomers to the restaurant business, but their barbecue has the well-cooked, smoked taste associated with the long established pork houses around the state. The menu is rounded out with a respectable variety of pork/beef hash, rice, pickles, loaf bread, and sweet tea. As the business grows, the Jessies plan to expand the menu to include such traditional Southern dishes as fried chicken.

THE PLACE:

     The Barbecue Diner offers "barracks barbecue" at its best. Leroy Jessie has an eye for a bargain and bought a surplus army barracks from nearby Fort Gordon to house his business. A few lighting changes and some personal flourishes Carrie Jessie supplied make this one of the most unusual settings for the serving of barbecue. The restaurant currently seats only 25-30 customers, but the building will allow the Jessies plenty of room for expansion as their business grows.

* * * * * * *

COUNTRY PIT BAR-B-QUE

LOCATION: Atomic Rd. (Hwy. 125) North Augusta 279-7546

HOURS: Every day 10 a.m. - 10 p.m.

TYPE: Regular menu and take-out

PRICES: Dinners-high; bulk rates-high

COOKING
TECHNIQUE: Open pit - oak and charcoal

THE BARBECUE:

     Ralph Gunnells and Dan Edwins gave up patrol cars for full time positions near the pits when they opened the Country Pit in May 1979. The former sheriff's department employees have turned a part-time hobby into a full time job. Staying open seven days a week is a rarity in the barbecue business, but Gunnells and Edwins seem to be managing things just fine. They pit-cook pork four times every week, allowing up to 12 hours' cooking time in the preparation of the hams and Boston butts. The ribs, chopped pork, beef and chicken barbecue served at the Country Pit were palatable but the key to good taste at the Country Pit was found in their sauces. The pork has already been sauced with a vinegar/spice mixture before reaching the customer. Diners are then left to choose from a mild or hot sauce offered as table selections. The mild sauce had a strong vinegar flavor that accented the pork taste. The hot sauce was more tangy than hot. When used sparingly, either sauce will richly enhance the otherwise typical pork. Chicken is served to customers only after the cooked poultry has been drenched with a rich, thick ketchup-based sauce. The chickens are placed on steam tables to allow the sauce to soak into the meat, resulting in a moist, tangy taste. Patrons can add to that tanginess by applying a peppery "chicken sauce" found on the tables in the restaurant. The Country Pit offers a full fare menu in addition to their barbecue entrees. Preparation of all food is carefully supervised by the owners, and both men make an honest effort to solicit customer comments.

THE PLACE:

     Gunnells and Edwins seem to have spared no expense in the outfitting of their restaurant.

Carpeting, wood paneling, decorative exposed beams, and a gleaming stainless salad bar are the highlights of the rich wood decor. Country Pit has enough comfortable wooden tables and chairs to seat 100 customers, and the rough wood exterior of the building almost suggests to passing motorists that wood-cooked barbecue is available inside.

* * * * * * *

LEE'S BAR-B-Q

LOCATION: 701 E. Buena Vista (2 blocks north of Hwy. 25 business route), North Augusta 279-6094

HOURS: Thurs.-Sat. 8 a.m. - 12 p.m.

TYPE: Located in a small, neighborhood bar, most business is take-out

PRICES: Dinners-average; bulk rates-average

COOKING
TECHNIQUE: Open pit - oak

THE BARBECUE:

Pit-cooked barbecue has turned up in some strange places over the centuries. Lee Alfred sells his oak-cooked pork over the bar at his neighborhood drinking establishment. Lee and his wife Lillie run a tiny bar-barbecue business in the Black residential district of North Augusta. Lee is a third generation pit tender, having learned his trade from his father and grandfather. Cooking his pork on a small pit over glowing coals, Alfred believes in turning the hams, shoulders and ribs frequently during their preparation. He chops or slices the meat to order, serving customers the unsauced pork with a sampling of his mustard-based hot barbecue sauce (sauce can be purchased). Without sauce, the pork's natural juices seemed to be released, producing a most enjoyable pork taste. A word to the wise: Alfred's sauce is one of the hottest mixtures in South Carolina and should be used very sparingly. Lee's Bar-B-Q specializes in barbecue, and their menu is limited to those few items.

THE PLACE:

Lee Alfred's bar is dimly lit, wood-paneled and offers very limited seating. A few booths and counter seats are usually filled with bar customers, so the best course of action may be to settle for a take-out sample of Alfred's pork. Lee Alfred mans the bar, cooks the barbecue and supplies most of the casual conversation found in this unique setting for a barbecue business.

* * * * * * *

BLACK'S BAR-B-Q

LOCATION:	Hwy. 70, 2-1/2 miles east of Barnwell 259-3767
HOURS:	Thurs.-Sat. 11 a.m. - 9:30 p.m.
TYPE:	Buffet, take-out and catering
PRICES:	Buffet low-average; bulk rates-average
COOKING TECHNIQUE:	Electric cooker - hickory smoker

THE BARBECUE:

    Emmet and Frankie Black opened their restaurant in October 1978. Emmet's father taught his son the tricks of the trade, and Emmet cut his teeth in the business by preparing huge barbecue feasts for church socials and family gatherings. When he was sure his recipe was ready, he opened the doors of this homey little restaurant. Black cooks his pork hams for 8-1/2 hours in eletric cookers, smoking the meat with hickory sticks. The barbecue is lean and flaky - a respectable version of electric-cooked pork. The buffet (all-you-can-eat) is a potpourri of barbecue side orders and includes BBQ beans, slaw, sweet pickles, pork-beef hash, chicken (fried) and iced tea. Black offers his customers a ketchup/mustard sauce (very tangy) and makes it available by the pint.

THE PLACE:

    Black's is located in a cement block building (his own design) located right on Hwy. 70 near Barnwell. Inside, the walls are paneled and decorated with Frankie Black's simple, homey adornments. The buffet is located on the back wall of the dining area which seats about 55 customers.

* * * * * * *

BO-CORLEY'S BAR-B-Q

LOCATION: 1617 Jackson St. (Hwy 64), Barnwell
259-3550

HOURS: Fri.-Sat. 11 a.m. - 9 p.m.

TYPE: Regular menu, take-out and catering

PRICES: Dinners-average; bulk rates-average

COOKING
TECHNIQUE: Combination gas/charcoal pit

THE BARBECUE:

    A.E. Corley has been cooking his barbecue in the same location for 11 years. Five years ago, Corley switched from open pit cooking to the gas/charcoal pit he now employs. Two cooks prepare 30-35 hams every week to meet the local demand for this barbecue. The finely chopped, pork had a charcoal smoked taste that was accented by Corley's special vinegar-based sauce. This sauce is applied to the hams late in the 9 hour cooking process. The Corley hash rated special attention, as it is a pork and beef mixture that had a delicious, mild onion taste. Chickens at Corley's are cooked, then immersed in a thick, ketchup-based sauce. The result is barbecued chicken that was tangy on the outside, tender on inside.

THE PLACE:

    A ramshackle white and red building serves as the home for Corley's barbecue restaurant. Stuffed with old diner furnishings, the restaurant can seat around 50 people. Yellow cement block construction provides a bright setting for customers who have come to enjoy "Bo" Corley's wares.

* * * * * * *

METTS' BAR-B-Q

LOCATION: Hwy. 301 on the south end of Bamberg
            245-4129

HOURS: Fri.-Sat. 11 a.m. - 8 p.m.

TYPE: Regular menu and take-out

PRICES: Dinners-low to average; bulk rates-average

COOKING
TECHNIQUE: Gas

THE BARBECUE:

Started by C.E. Metts, Sr., this tiny restaurant has changed hands within the family and is currently owned by C.E. Metts, Jr. For over 15 years, Mrs. C.E. Metts, Sr., has been working with husband and/or son in the restaurant, and the spry older woman still tends to the barbecue appetites of her Bamberg friends and customers. The Metts menu is simple. Chopped barbecue is the house special, coming to the customers after the pork shoulders have had a 10 hour stint in the gas oven. The meat is finely chopped, then sauced with a mustard/ketchup/vinegar/spice sauce. The chopped barbecue was a chewy, heavily sauced brand of pork. Barbecued chicken at Metts means oven-cooked poultry served beneath a thin basting of the same sauce used on the pork. Pork hash was an onion and potato blend that is made from the meat of Boston butts. A complete sandwich menu is available, offering customers an alternative to pork barbecue.

THE PLACE:

Adjacent to a service garage/filling station, Metts is a shoe-box sized restaurant. The restaurant seems to borrow some of the dingy cast of the garage. A few tables and booths provide seating for up to 25 patrons, and customer orders are taken at the back of the dining area. Metts serves primarily take-out orders.

* * * * * * *

ED NEELEY'S BAR-B-Q

LOCATION: Hwy. 321 at the Sweden crossroads, Denmark
                 793-3133

HOURS: Fri. and Sat. 11 a.m. - 9 p.m.

TYPE: Buffet, take-out and catering

PRICES: Buffet-low; bulk rates-average

COOKING
TECHNIQUE: Electric cooker - hickory-smoked

THE BARBECUE:

     Phil Neely is the third generation member of his family to try his hand at the barbecue business. For over 23 yars the Neeley name has been associated with the tiny restaurant on Hwy. 321, and barbecue has always been the mainstay on the menu. Neeley's barbecued pork is sauced twice before it ever reaches the consumer. During cooking, a primary sauce (that Neeley claims gives his pork its true barbecue flavor) is applied. After cooking, the pork is chipped, and a mild ketchup/mustard-based sauce is added to enhance the barbecue flavor. Neeley then offers his customers a tangy mustard-based table sauce. The cooked pork was finely chipped, fat-free and highly sauced. Barbecued chicken is available upon request, but customers must wait approximately one-half hour before being served. Neeley oven-bakes his chicken, then dips whole chickens in a butter/lemon/vinegar sauce to achieve a barbecue taste. Hash, made with 2/3 pork and 1/3 beef, was a very smooth, slightly oniony sampling of the traditional barbecue fare. Of special note are the hush puppies at Neeley's. These corn meal puppies are offered two ways - with or without onions - and both varieties had a delicious buttery flavor. Pork skins, potato salad and sweet pickles round out the all-you-can-eat buffet. Phil Neeley says he has served people from "Alaska, England, and California, but mostly just good Eastern Seaboard folks."

THE PLACE:

     Perched right on the edge of Hwy. 321, Neeley's offers customers a diner-type atmosphere and can seat up to 85 persons. The low-ceilinged, squat building provides a quaint, quiet setting for Phil

Neeley's stories about life on the Edisto River. The long, narrow diner is also a showcase for the work of local artists, and the proprietor keeps a guest register handy for the customer to sign. Neeley's location brings many truckers and vacationing tourists thorugh the narrow doorway.

* * * * * * *

DUKES BBQ

LOCATION:	Hwy. 321 on the north end of town in Fairfax
HOURS:	Tues.-Thurs. 11:30 a.m. - 2 p.m. and Fri. -Sat. 11 a.m. - 9 p.m.
TYPE:	Buffet and take-out
PRICES:	Buffet-low; dinners-average; bulk rates-average
COOKING TECHNIQUE:	Would not reveal preparation method

THE BARBECUE:

Employees of the Duke's location in Fairfax were reluctant to say anything about the business during the owner's absence. The all-you-can-eat buffet included chopped pork, hash and rice, slaw, pickles, loaf bread, and iced tea.

THE PLACE:

An inauspicious red brick building houses this Duke's BBQ. Large picture windows at the front entrance help to make the main dining area a brightly lighted one. The dining room is clean, and a stainless steel buffet line at the rear allows the customers easy access to the buffet fare. Long, narrow tables and benches provide seating for 40-50 customers.

NORTH CENTRAL REGION

****

DAVID BROWN'S HICKORY HOUSE PIT BAR-B-Q

LOCATION: Located where Hwy. 321 Business and Hwy. 321 By-Pass split at the southern edge of Winnsboro 635-4324

HOURS: Thurs.-Sat. 10 a.m. - 10 p.m.

TYPE: Regular menu, take-out and catering (with plans to move toward a buffet)

PRICES: Dinners-average; bulk rates-average

COOKING
TECHNIQUE: Closed pit - indirect heat from hickory

THE BARBECUE:

     David Brown has been in the barbecue business less than three months, but already he has established himself as a barbecue man par excellence. A traveling salesman-turned barbecue owner, Brown has brought top quality barbecue to the north central region of the state. The smoker pit Brown uses is an improvisation on a pit he saw a man using in Blackstock, South Carolina, several years ago. Brown expanded on that pit, creating a hickory-fueled smoking pit that is fed a constant supply of wood smoke from two fireboxes located on the rear of the building.

     Brown cooks whole hogs 12-14 hours (depending on the size of the hogs) and uses low-country vinegar-based sauce in the preparation of his chopped barbecue. Brown says his choice of the vinegar/pepper sauce is evidence of his belief in his barbecue. "I don't try to cover up the taste of my meat with ketchup or mustard. I want people to taste the real thing." The "real thing" Brown cooks is second to none in this region of the state. The chopped pork was the leanest, moistest, hickory-smokiest barbecue in the area. The owner says the leanness of his pork is testimony to the fact that he cooks his pork slowly. According to Brown, "Sauce will cover up anything, but you don't need a good sauce if you sell a good barbecue." Brown does.

Besides the chopped pork, ribs, beef/pork hash, mayonnaise and vinegar slaws, chicken bog and Brunswick stew round out Brown's menu, but the focal point of the menu is the chopped pork. David Brown and helper Danny Evans prepare pork barbecue that is certain to make their business grow into the buffet restaurant Brown envisions the business will become.

THE PLACE:

A single smoke stack rising above a neatly trimmed brown and white building will guide barbecue lovers to this meaty mecca. While Brown's business has limited dine-in facilities (2 picnic tables will seat about 12 people), he has definite plans for an adjoining dining room in the very near future. The closed pit Brown uses gives the building a faint hickory aroma. The "Hickory House" is clean-scrubbed, cement floored, and staffed with some of the friendliest, good country people you could ever hope to meet.

* * * * * * *

WESTWOOD BAR-B-Q

LOCATION: 151 By-Pass, 1-1/2 miles west of Hwy. 15, Hartsville 332-7142

HOURS: Thurs.-Sat. 11 a.m. - 9 p.m.

TYPE: Buffet, take-out and catering

PRICES: Buffet-average; bulk rates-average

COOKING
TECHNIQUE: Electric

THE BARBECUE:

In 1947 Arnold Fowler helped a friend open Respies Barbecue in Greenville, South Carolina. Working for A&P, Mr. Fowler was quite familiar with choosing the best cuts of meat and other preparation techniques. In 1967 he brought together his ideas about barbecuing and knowledge of the meat business when he opened Westwood Bar-B-Q. He admitted to the similarity between the eastern North Carolina style barbecue he helped his friend prepare and the South Carolina barbecue he now cooks. Using electric pits, Mr. Fowler cooks pork, chicken and beef ribs. Very secretive about cooking techniques and sauce ingredients, the proprietor did confess that the special taste of his barbecue depended on the way he salted the meat, the sauce recipe and the mixing ratio of sauce to pork. The all-you-can-eat lunch buffet consists of a variety of barbecued items as well as specialty dishes: chopped pork barbecue, beef ribs, barbecued chicken, rice and red hash gravy (made with pork and beef), liver hash, fried chicken, homemade hush puppies, two kinds of cole slaw, sweet pickles and white loaf bread. The evening buffet, priced a little higher, also includes dried pork skins and chicken livers and gizzards.

The finely chopped barbecue was very lean and delicately seasoned with Fowler's tangy mustard sauce. The beef ribs, meaty and juicy, were drenched in a spicy tomato-based sauce. The mustard sauce and the hot tomato sauce (which have 35-year-old recipes that only Fowler knows) can be purchased by the pint. Sauced as much as the ribs was the chicken, which was juicy and tender to the falling-off-the-bone point. Seasoned well with tomatoes and spices, the red hash gravy is an unusual dish for this area. For his three day business, Fowler fixes 75 gallons a week. Soon to be added to Westwood's fare is a specialty item found mostly in Texas and the West: boneless barbecue beef briskets.

THE PLACE:

Westwood Bar-B-Q sits between a set of railroad tracks and a vacant lot on Hwy. 151 By-Pass. The nondescript white building has an eye-catching pig weather vane over the front door. Directly in front of the entrance way is the take-out counter where one can order anything from a buffet plate to five pounds of beef ribs to go. A large lighted Coke machine stands to the left beside the cash register and check-out counter. Although the interior is somewhat plain, there is some warmth in the green patterned carpet and the homey lighting fixtures. The 145-seating dining room is furnished mostly with wooden tables and ladder-back chairs. Quite noticeably on one light green cement-block wall are two plaques: one of a U.S.C. gamecock and the other of a Clemson tiger. Because it is decorated like a covered wagon, the buffet stands out well.

* * * * * * *

MIDWAY BBQ

LOCATION: Buffalo Rd. (Hwy. 215 West), Union
             427-4047

HOURS: Thurs.-Sat. 9 a.m. - 9 p.m.
             (Jack Odell soon plans to open 5-6 days
             a week, also serving sliced barbecue,
             ribs, chicken and beef).

TYPE: Regular menu and take-out (The restaurant
             is set-up for take-out)

PRICES: Dinners-low; bulk rates-average.

COOKING
TECHNIQUE: Open pit - hickory

THE BARBECUE:

Although Midway BBQ is only eight years old, owner Jack Odell has been cooking barbecue for over 38 years. To open on Thursday, Odell kindles the hickory wood fires on Tuesday and piles hams and shoulders to cook for 16-20 hours. Quite reluctant to divulge exact cooking procedures, Mr. Odell did admit that he cooks the meat fat-side-up until almost done and then turns the meat. He applies no sauce to the pork as it cooks but serves a tomato-based sauce with each helping. For special occasions a vinegar and pepper sauce is available. Lean and moist, Odell's barbecue ranks among the top five in hotness of seasoning - definitely a two-Coke barbecue. From the larger chunks of meat emerges a sweet hickory flavor. A stainless steel drum kept under constant heat in boiling water holds one of Odell's specialities: hash - a treat for those who like theirs spicy and oniony. According to the owner, "The native dish is hash - the people around here love it!" Another popular item is Odell's chicken stew, a pepper-laced recipe with chunks of tender chicken in a milk base. Served with each order are sweet pickles and store-bought buns or white loaf bread. The customer may purchase a beverage from a drink machine near the order counter.

THE PLACE:

As with many bona fide barbecue establishments, Midway's offers little "atmosphere" as most people know it. But this place is a treat for those who enjoy offbeat places with plenty of character and color: low, screened, ramshackled building; dingy walls; huge galvanized trash cans inside and out; concrete and sawdust covered floors; and old kitchen tables (seating about 6). Adjacent to the barbecue-serving area is a meat market that sells freshly cut pork, beef, liver mush, homemade sausage and slab bacon.

* * * * * * *

BUDDY'S HICKORY COOKED BAR-B-Q

LOCATION:	Hwy. 72 & 121 in Chester 385-5641
HOURS:	Phone weekdays between 8 a.m. and 5 p.m.
TYPE:	Wholesale and catering
PRICES:	Uncertain
COOKING TECHNIQUE:	Hickory cooked

THE BARBECUE:

Buddy's barbecue is prepared in a building adjacent to the old drive-in facility which is now the home of "Studio 72" disco and is available only on a wholesale basis and for catered parties.

* * * * * * *

FAT WILLY'S HAWG HOUSE

LOCATION:	1)	Carowinds Boulevard right off I-77 Fort Mill 548-4989
	2)	1158 Cherry Rd., Rock Hill 366-5181
HOURS:	1)	Mon.-Thurs. 11 a.m. - 9 p.m.; Fri.-Sat. 11 a.m. - 12 p.m.
	2)	Tues.-Wed. 11 a.m. - 3 p.m. Thurs.-Sat. 11 a.m. - 9 p.m.
TYPE:		Regular menu and take-out
PRICES:		Dinners-average; bulk rates-high
COOKING TECHNIQUE:		Electric roticery - hickory-smoked

THE BARBECUE:

Jord "Fat Willy" Jordan had long dreamed of the day when he would own a barbecue establishment.

Today he owns three of them. Jordan has been cooking barbecue over 25 years. Three years ago he opened his first Fat Willy's in Charlotte, North Carolina, and they have since been moving steadily south. Fat Willy's pork is cooked over 12 hours and the resulting sliced meat is delicious. Beef, pork, or chicken; Fat Willy's barbecue offers hickory-smoked, consistently good taste. The meat was somewhat chewy and is delivered unsauced. Fat Willy's barbecue offers his customers three sauces: mustard-based (with honey), hot tomato-based (using Chinese hot peppers), and a mild, sweet tomato-based mixture. All sauces are rich in taste and, when used sparingly, accent the rich smoked taste of the barbecued meats. Barbecue plates are served with a choice of two side dishes from the following list: BBQ beans, Brunswick stew, french fries, cole slaw or chili. Hush puppies are served on the plates. The Fat Willy's location on Carowinds Bouelvard offers customers the option of enjoying their favorite mixed drinks with dinner, and the Rock Hill location has cold beer on tap. For selection, Fat Willy's ranks high on the list of barbecue establishments. The Fat Willy's menu offers something for the non-barbecue lover and, for fast-service barbecue, it ranks among the best.

THE PLACE:

     Fat Willy's locations are as gray as the hickory coals that smoke the meat. The Carowinds location offers booth and table seating for over 125 customers, and the dining area is spacious. The Rock Hill location is a converted fish and chip restaurant, and swivel seats in the small dining area will seat up to 40 customers.

* * * * * * *

WILLARD'S BBQ AND HASH HOUSE

LOCATION: 416 Pecan St. (near Chandler Dr., off Hwy. 18), Gaffney   489-1291

HOURS: Thurs.-Sat. 8:30 a.m. - 8 p.m.

TYPE: Regular menu, take-out and catering

PRICE: Dinners-average.

COOKING
TECHNIQUE: Electric

THE BARBECUE:

     Mr. Billie Willard's family has operated Willard's BBQ for 12 years. Boned and rolled hams are cooked slowly for 24-26 hours over and under electrical units that go on and off every 14 seconds. The result is chopped and sliced barbecued pork that was somewhat dry. The barbecue hash seems to be quite popular with Mr. Willard's customers. It was juicy and onion-laced, but not overbearing. A full menu, including fried chicken, fish, and shrimp, is offered. Mr. Willard, quite proud of his barbecue, remarked, "I had to learn the hard way - I threw a lot away."

THE PLACE:

The cement-block, concrete-floored building contains small tables, folding chairs and an antiquated console television. Photographs of long lines of people waiting to buy hash on the 4th-of-Julys-past nearly fill one wall. This main dining room seats 35-40, and a large room in the back can accommodate 100. A walk-up window gives customers the option of a fast-food approach.

* * * * * * *

HILLTOP RESTAURANT

LOCATION: Hwy. 21 South - 1-1/2 miles south of Great Falls 482-4778

HOURS: Tues.-Wed. 7 a.m. - 11 p.m.;
Thurs.-Fri. 7 a.m. - 2 a.m.;
Sat. 8 a.m. - 2 p.m.

TYPE: Regular menu, take-out and catering

PRICE: Dinners-average; bulk rates-average

COOKING
TECHNIQUE: Open pit - hickory

THE BARBECUE:

With the restaurant having been open only since February 1978, owner Donald Young is very pleased with the barbecue sales at Hilltop. On an open brick-pit not too far from the restaurant, he cooks Boston butts for 18-26 hours over hickory. No sauce is applied until the pork is chopped and ready to be served. The stringy, minced barbecue had a pleasant hickory taste that was not overridden by the sauce. Only 1-1/2 years old, the sauce recipe is a pepper-laced, mustard/ketchup (more ketchup than mustard, it seemed) combination. On the barbecue plate french fries, hush puppies, and slaw are added. Sandwiches, seafood, steaks, and chicken make up the rest of the restaurant's fare.

THE PLACE:

      Hilltop Restaurant is a white-painted brick building standing beside an Exxon station. A neon sign outside advertises "pit cooked BBQ." Inside are a game room with pinball machines and a dining room with a loud-playing jukebox. Seven booths line the papered walls. Several large tables with chairs occupy the center dining area. The local customers seat themselves at the long counter, behind which the food is prepared. The pleasant employees and the friendly diner atmosphere of the Hilltop make the customers feel welcome here.

                    * * * * * * *

BONEY'S BAR-B-QUE

LOCATION: Off Hwy. 21 on Ruff St., Ridgeway 337-2675

HOURS: Boney's serves barbecue only on Fri. and Sat., but it is open, serving other food, Mon.-Sat. 10 a.m. - late evenings

TYPE: Take-out only

PRICE: Dinners-average; bulk rates-low

COOKING
TECHNIQUE: Open pit - hickory and oak

THE BARBECUE:

      Iley and James Lee Boney, third generation barbecue cookers, have been operating for three years. The Boneys begin cooking their pork (Boston butts) and chicken at 2 a.m. Friday. After burning the wood outside for about an hour and a half, Mr. Boney shovels the coals into the pits inside the screened shed. He cooks the pork about 7-1/2 to 8 hours, turning it one time about two-thirds through the process. The pork is chopped into large, crusty-edged chunks that had a salty, smoked flavor. The chicken was meaty and had a delicious smoked taste. The Boney's tangy mustard-based sauce accents the hickory smoke flavor. Another specialty the Boneys are proud of is their beef hash (3rd generation recipe), which had a juicy, oniony taste. Says Mr. Boney, "I learn a little bit more every time I cook."

THE PLACE:

      Boney's barbecue is little more than a screened shed. Inside there is room for only about

-96-

four customers at a time. A formica counter separates the customers from the blackened pits. A meat saw (resembling a hack saw) hangs above the cement floor. Outside on the postage-stamp lot are a red picnic table, several large trash barrels and a pile of hickory and oak. Iley and James Boney are loquacious, friendly people who enjoy seeing their customers' hungers satisfied with their generous servings of barbecue.

* * * * * * *

BROOME'S RESTAURANT

LOCATION: Camden Hwy. (Hwy. 601), Kershaw 475-2575

HOURS: Tues.-Sat. 11 a.m. - 11 p.m.;
Sun. 6:30 a.m. - 11 p. m.

TYPE: Regular menu, take-out, curb service and catering

PRICE: Dinners-average; bulk rates-average

COOKING
TECHNIQUE: Open pit - hickory

THE BARBECUE:

Although the restaurant has been open for seven years, Billy and Donna Broome have been serving barbecue only during the last three. The couple cook hams for 12 hours, turning and basting them frequently. The mild sauce is a blend of ketchup and mustard. Two varieties of pork are offered: minced and sliced. The Broomes mentioned that they occasionally serve a barbecue buffet which includes ribs, chicken and pork. A homemade pork hash is also on the menu, along with seafood, steaks and sandwiches.

THE PLACE:

A large dining room, carpeted and furnished with red and black decor, seats 125 customers. A small room off to the side contains a counter and stools. A large lighted sign illuminates the brick exterior of Broome's.

* * * * * * *

LITTLE BETSY'S BAR-B-Q RESTAURANT

LOCATION: Hwy. 151 East, McBee   335-8448

HOURS: Every day 5 a.m. - about 8 p.m.;
               Sept.-March, closed Tuesdays

TYPE: Regular menu and take-out

PRICE: Dinners-high; bulk rates-low

COOKING
TECHNIQUE: Open pit - oak

THE BARBECUE:

     Twenty-four years ago Betsy and Gary Sullivan opened their restaurant and began serving hot dogs and hamburgers to tourists heading for the beach or for Darlington Speedway. Mrs. Sullivan had done very little cooking until then. Three years later her husband built a 300-pound capacity cement-block barbecue pit. Today, although they have greatly expanded their menu, the Sullivans do a tremendous barbecue business. Cooking begins Wednesday about 4 a.m. Oak is burned outside and the coals brought inside to the pit. The Sullivans have gone from cooking shoulders to cooking hams, and now they use only Boston butts. They are cooked four or five hours, then chopped or sliced. In a stainless steel tub Mrs. Sullivan places alternating layers of sauce and meat. Then it is reheated on a steam table to bring out the smoked flavor. The sliced barbecue consisted of somewhat fatty, well-peppered chunks of pork with a strong smoked taste. The chopped barbecue had an even stronger smoked taste. One sauce, developed over 20 years ago through trial and error, is served. In addition to Worchestershire sauce, brown sugar, vinegar, tomato juice, mustard, Texas Pete, lemon juice, salt and pepper, it has Stokely's Ketchup -- a MUST for the rich taste Betsy Sullivan wants her sauce to have. Various non-barbecue entrees are also on the menu.

THE PLACE:

     Little Betsy's has a typical diner-type interior, with small formica-topped tables and padded chairs (seating 65) arranged throughout the two dining rooms. Glass or crystal chandeliers seem rather out-of-place in the wood-paneled, slate-floored room. Bamboo shades and hanging plants decorate the large windows that overlook the parking area and highway. The exterior is brick with white metal awnings. Beside the restaurant is Little Betsy's fruit and vegetable stand.

* * * * * * *

SHILOH BBQ

<u>LOCATION</u>:	5 miles south of Hwy. 9 on S.C. 102 - Shiloh Community, Chesterfield 623-6380
<u>HOURS</u>:	Fri. and Sat. 4 p.m. - 10 p.m.
<u>TYPE</u>:	Regular menu and take-out
<u>PRICE</u>:	Dinners-average; bulk rates-average
<u>COOKING TECHNIQUE</u>:	Electric cooker - oak-smoked

<u>THE BARBECUE</u>:

    Ralph and Geraldine Watson introduced barbecue to their fish camp customers 12 years ago. Demand for their pork warranted their opening Shiloh BBQ in December 1978. Shiloh serves three types of barbecue: pork, chicken and beef ribs. The Watsons use only locally-bought hams and shoulders for their chopped barbecue. After about 7 hours of electric cooking, the meat is smoked for 2 hours. Black-jack oak is used for this segment of the cooking cycle. A distinct smoked flavor permeates the lean, chunky meat which is prepared and served without sauce. Customers may help themselves, according to individual preferences, to the Watsons' homemade sauce. Containing plenty of vinegar and pepper, it compliments the pork without obscuring the smoked taste. A thicker, more tomatoey sauce is used to baste the chicken and ribs. While lacking a smoked taste, the chicken was tender and evenly cooked. The ribs were large and meaty. Shiloh's other specialties include liver hash, cinnamon-flavor candied yams, crunchy cole slaw and hot cornbread sticks. A selection of non-barbecue entrees is available.

<u>THE PLACE</u>:

    Built in 1978, Shiloh's building is tastefully furnished with original artwork (created by the Watsons' artist-daughter), simple tables and chairs, and a subdued color scheme. The restaurant seats 40-50 customers.

* * * * * * *

REVEL'S BARBECUE CENTER

LOCATION: Hwy. 15/401, 1-1/2 miles north of Bennettsville
                  479-2046

HOURS: Mon.-Sat. 9 a.m. - 10 p.m.;
                  Sun. 9 a.m. - 3 p.m.

TYPE: Regular menu and take-out (buffet luncheon)

PRICE: Dinners-high; buffet-high; bulk rates-average

COOKING
TECHNIQUE: Electric

THE BARBECUE:

     Revel's Barbecue Center is located behind the old Revel's Restaurant (no longer run by the Revel family). The Barbecue Center is the home of the Revels' wholesale processing plant. Mr. Revel started this enterprise over 65 years ago. His wife continued to run the restaurant-end of the business for some time after Mr. Revel's death, but has since leased the rstaurant, and turned over the running of the family wholesale operation to her son-in-law Rochell Carroll. In the restaurant, Revel's barbecue is still served. Barbecue plates in the restaurant are served with french fries, cole slaw, and rolls or hush puppies.

     The wholesale operation is impressive. Carroll uses four Bar-B-Q Slave cookers to prepare his meat for supermarket and restaurant sales. Shoulders and hams are cooked 6-1/2 to 7-1/2 hours, after which the meat is chopped or sliced, sauced with Revel's vinegar and ketchup-based sauce (a 65 year-old recipe), and packed in containers for delivery to wholesale customers. Revel's slaw is also distributed to retail outlets. The slaw is a strong mayonnaise and vinegar recipe that is prepared in the same facility.

THE PLACE:

     Revel's restaurant is a brick building set on the edge of the McColl highway just north of Bennettsville. Inside the rambling brick structure, customers can choose table or booth seats. Revel's is a huge restaurant with seating for over 250 people. The walls are adorned with fish nets, mounted fish, and an "fish camp" decorator items. Revel's wholesale plant offers stark white walls, scrubbed floors, stainless steel tables and an abundance of processing equipment.

* * * * * * *

REYNOLD'S BAR-B-Q

LOCATION: 129 East DeKalb St. (Hwy. 1), downtown
                   Camden 432-9521

HOURS: Mon.-Sat. 11 a.m. - 9 p.m.

TYPE: Regular menu and take-out

PRICE: Dinners-average; bulk rates-average

COOKING
TECHNIQUE: Electric cooker - hickory-smoked

THE BARBECUE:

      John M. and Fannie Reynolds have operated Reynold's Bar-B-Q since 1972. They cook unbasted hams for about 12 hours on an electric cooker with hickory smoker attached. Their other barbecued meats include pork ribs, chicken and hash. The finely chopped barbecued pork had a hickory aroma and flavor, and just a little sweet sauce had been added to the moist meat. The sauce, only an 8-year-old recipe, contained both mustard and ketchup, but the ketchup taste was dominant. Both the chicken and the meaty ribs had been lightly sauced as they cooked. (Barbecued chicken is served only on Friday and Saturday at Reynold's). Homemade hush puppies (with a slight onion flavor) are served with the plates.

THE PLACE:

      The barbecue establishment looks out upon busy DeKalb Street and a parking lot is provided off the street, beside the restaurant. This glass front, bricked building contains seating for 50 at simple tables and chairs scattered throughout the small dining room.

* * * * * * *

HAMMY'S BAR-B-Q HOUSE

LOCATION: U.S. 1, Elgin (about 20 miles form Columbia)
              438-3249

HOURS: Fri.-Sat. 11 a.m. - 9:30 p.m.;
              Labor Day: 4th of July

TYPE: Buffet, take-out and catering

PRICE: Buffet-average; bulk rates-average

COOKING
TECHNIQUE: Electric-cooked first; then wood-smoked
              on an open pit

THE BARBECUE:

Andrea and Diane Moak opened Hammy's in September 1969. For the first 4-5 years they cooked only with wood, but they soon switched to an electric cooker. The meat is cooked for a total of 12-15 hours, first on the electric pit and then on the hickory and oak pit to produce the smoked flavor. The meat is mixed with a mild mustard sauce after it has been chopped. Only the beef ribs are served with a tomato-based sauce. On the all-you-can-eat buffet a variety of barbecue items is offered: chopped pork (from hams), pork and beef ribs and barbecued chicken. The chopped barbecue (the string type) was lean, moist and lightly flavored with wood smoke. The beef ribs were quite well done and had a trace of sauce flavor. The juicy pork ribs, on the other hand, were smothered in a mildly spicy mustard sauce that did not overshadow the taste of the meat. Tender and lightly basted, the chic- ken was a little bland. The beef hash had a pleasant, lightly seasoned taste. Served with the buffet are potato salad, baked beans, corn on the cob, slaw, pickles, chicken bog, pork skins (crisp and lightly salted), white loaf bread, tea and lemonade.

THE PLACE:

The wood and brick building contains one open dining room filled with long metal tables and chairs -ideal for large groups - with a seating capacity of 110. On each oil cloth-covered table are bottles of barbecue sauce and Texas Pete hot sauce. A stainless steel buffet holds the food.

* * * * * * *

WARD'S BAR-B-Q

LOCATION:
1) 617 Boulevard Rd. (Hwy. 15), Sumter 775-9864
   Thurs.-Sat. 10:30 a.m. - 7:30 p.m.

2) 416 E. Liberty St., Sumter 775-1490
   Thurs.-Sat. 10:30 a.m. - 7:30 p.m.

3) 614 Manning St., Sumter 773-1338
   Every day 10 a.m. - 9 p.m.

4) Alice Dr. and Hwy. 76, Sumter 469-8400
   Thurs.-Sat. 10:30 a.m. - 7:30 p.m.

5) 2-1/2 miles from Columbia's VA Hospital on Hwy. 378 783-2548
   Thurs.-Sat. 10:30 a.m. - 7:30 p.m.

TYPE: Take-out and catering

PRICE: Dinners-low; bulk rates-average

COOKING TECHNIQUE: Electric cooker - hickory-smoked

THE BARBECUE:

      The first barbecue place opened by owner Thad Ward, Jr., was one on Boulevard Rd. in 1954. Gradually he expanded his business, opening three other "drive-in, take-out" places in Sumter and one just a few months ago on Hwy. 378 almost to Columbia. Three more Ward's Bar-B-Q's for the Columbia area are in the works now. For the first seventeen years Thad Ward cooked with wood on an open pit, but there was such demand for his barbecue that he was forced to switch to an electric cooker. Now all the barbecuing is done on seven electric pits at one location - the original place on Boulevard Rd. He distributes his barbecue to all other locations. Cooking 3,000-4,000 pounds of barbecue per week requires the assistance of four employees. They load the pits with whole hogs which are cooked for 6-7 hours and hickory-smoked part of that time. Not until the pork is 30 minutes from being ready is it sauced.

      The fifty-year-old sauce recipe includes a large quantity of black and red pepper in a hot, vinegary base. Ward's Original Pork and Beef Bar-B-Q Hot

Sauce, which he sells to his customers by the pint and by the quart, contains hickory-smoke flavoring to give the meat a little zest. The sauce goes well with chicken, pork or beef ribs. Lean and moist, the chopped pork had no distinct hickory flavor by itself, but the liquid smoke in the sauce provided a hint of it. Surprisingly, it was difficult to tell the artificial hickory flavor from the natural. The beef ribs were crusty, lean and chewy. The sauce on the tender chicken was a little richer and more tomatoey than the regular barbecue sauce, but there was no trace of hickory in it. Another big-selling item on Ward's menu is the all-pork hash, a rich peppery dish with a tomato base. He also offers sandwiches, hamburgers and fried chicken.

THE PLACE:

All of Ward's places are similar in appearance. The large "W" painted on the windows is Thad Ward's trademark. The newest location in Sumter (614 Manning St.) is an old 1950's-looking building with drive-up and walk-up counter service. The menu is on the wall, and the customer can watch the order being prepared as he waits outside. The 416 E. Liberty location is a bit newer. There is no seating available.

* * * * * * *

BAR-B-Q HUT RESTAURANT

LOCATION: 1220 Pocallo Rd. (Hwy. 15) Sumter 773-8717

HOURS: Mon.-Sat. 11:30 a.m. - 2 p.m.

TYPE: Regular menu (cafeteria style), take-out and catering

PRICE: Dinners-low; bulk rates-average

COOKING
TECHNIQUE: Electric cooker - hickory-smoked

THE BARBECUE:

The Bar-B-Q Hut Restaurant has been owned and operated by Kenneth Young for twelve years. He cooks about 2,000 pounds of meat a week - only shoulders for his chopped barbecue because, he says, they are sweeter and jucier than other cuts of pork. One large pit can handle 300 pounds of meat for one cooking, which is usually six hours long (including two hours for hickory smoking). As it cooks, the meat is frequently basted. The tomato-based sauce, whose recipe is as old as the restaurant, is on the hot and spicy side. Its sweet taste did not, however, override the big hickory smoke flavor that was present in the large chunks of juicy barbecue. When asked to define barbecue, Mr. Young paused and then said firmly, "Barbecue is really your sauce." The meaty ribs are cooked with generous amount of the same hot tomato sauce. Baked and then dipped in a sweeter sauce, the chicken was moist and tender. Young's hash, made from 100% pork, had a sweet, tomatoey flavor. Other menu items are fresh vegetables, seafood and red chicken stew.

THE PLACE:

The Bar-B-Que Restaurant is actually two buildings that share the same kitchen. The carry-out side has a long counter and by-the-pound prices on the wall. The dining area, simply decorated, contains seating for 184 at large and medium-sized tables covered with red cloths. A sign reading "Hogs are beautiful" hangs over the management's corner.

* * * * * * *

D & H BAR-B-Q

LOCATION: 412 Mills St., downtown Manning 435-2189

HOURS: Wed.-Sat. 10 a.m. - 8 p.m.

TYPE: Regular menu, take-out and catering

PRICE: Dinners-average; bulk rates-average

COOKING
TECHNIQUE: Open pit - oak

THE BARBECUE:

D & H Bar-B-Q has been operating for 30 years. Owner John Denny still uses the original cooking method: he cooks whole hogs, unseasoned, over oak coals in a long brick pit behind the kitchen. He serves the barbecued pork in two ways: sliced and chopped. Also available are pork ribs, pork skins and sliced beef barbecue. The chopped pork had a slight smoked flavor, as well as a light taste of vinegar. (The table sauce has a vinegar base). The sliced pork, containing a little fat, had a stronger smoked flavor. The ribs were a little dry, with only a hint of any sauce. Pork hash and cole slaw are also on the menu at D & H.

THE PLACE:

The large green building has two sides to it: one for carry-out only and one for eating in. The dining room contains seating for about 50 customers at 8 picnic tables. A large Coke machine stands beside the walk-up order counter at the far end of the small room.

NORTHWEST REGION

SAWGRASS JIM'S BAR-B-Q HOUSE

LOCATION: 147 South Pine St., Spartanburg 582-1234
HOURS: Every day 10 a.m. - 9 p.m.
TYPE: Regular menu (cafeteria style) and take-out
PRICE: Dinners-average; bulk rates-high
COOKING
TECHNIQUE: Closed pit - indirect heat from hickory

THE BARBECUE:

Sawgrass Jim's was one of the most interesting barbecue places we visited because of his unique method of cooking and his variety of barbecued foods. Jimmy Howell, a member of a three-generation barbecuing family, has been cooking for his friends and relatives for 40 years. The story behind the name of his restaurant is intriguing. His father lived in Florida during Prohibition where Moonshiners built stills in the tall sawgrass of the swamps. If revenuers were in the vicinity, scouting for the illegal stills, the moonshiners quickly and cleverly converted their stills to barbecue pits. Thus, whenever a family gathered for a big barbecue, one could be sure that law enforcement officers were lurking in the area. On the opening day in December 1978, Jimmy Howell, commemorating these days of Florida sawgrass barbecue-fronts for whiskey-makers, named his place Sawgrass Jim's.

According to Mr. Howell, the cooking method he uses is ancient. He calls it "dry cured cooking," a technique that has Biblical and Indian documentation. Using this method requires a two-compartment oven, usually made of brick or concrete. The smaller compartment holds burning wood coals, which Mr. Howell obtains from green hickory. The smoke produced is drawn naturally through vents up and into the adjacent compartment, a large oven where the meat is hung or

-107-

placed on metal racks. Thus, the smoke, not the flames, from the burning hickory cooks the meat - indirectly. To make this barbecue, Jimmy Howell places whole hogs in the closed pit (500 pound capacity) and smokes them for 10-11 hours at about 190° - 195° F. Since the smoke can permeate the meat from all directions, no turning of the hogs is required. However, he does season the meat a little with dry spices while it is cooking.

"True smoked meat will be a pinkish color -all chicken, turkey, and pork is cooked well done," printed at the top of Sawgrass Jim's menu, is an explanation to customers who worry when they bite into some pink chicken and think it has not been cooked properly. All of the meat was juicy, lean and had a delicious hickory taste. The barbecued pork, finely chopped and not a bit greasy, tasted best with the mustard/vinegar sauce, but it also tasted good with both tomato-based ones (one hot, the other mild). Moist and succulent, the chicken had a sweet hickory flavor that was outstanding. The meaty pork ribs, hot pink on the inside, were a little disappointing because they were cooked with no sauce. Only the barbecue beef hash, simmered in a variety of dry spices, was prepared with sauce. Other smoked meats on the menu are Polish sausage, sliced beef, turkey (whole or breast) and hams. Side orders include Brunswick stew, barbecued beans, cole slaw, hush puppies and stewed potatoes.

THE PLACE:

Comfortable surroundings and the pleasant aroma of sweet hickory greet the customer of Sawgrass Jim's. The carpeted, wood-paneled dining room has soft booths, tables and chairs to seat 240. Basket plants hanging in front of the windows make the large room seem cozy. A detailed menu hangs above the buffet line. Service is through a cafeteria line, and the customer pays after he has chosen his food.

* * * * * * *

BEACON DRIVE-IN

LOCATION: 255 Reidville Rd., Spartanburg 585-9387

HOURS: Mon.-Sat. 7 a.m. - 11:30 p.m.

TYPE: Regular menu, take-out and catering

PRICES: Dinners-average; bulk rates-average

COOKING
TECHNIQUE: Electric - wood smoked

THE BARCECUE:

    When an out-of-towner visits Spartanburg for any length of time, he inevitably winds up feasting at the Beacon, a long-time institution there. John B. White, Sr., has owned and operated the Beacon, with the help of his sons, since 1947. Until about 1959 or 1960, he used wood-burning pits to barbecue his hogs. Now, especially with his ever-increasing catering business (a 13,000 people-feeder was the largest), Mr. White has had to switch to electric cookers with attached smokers: three large and one small manufactured by Barbecue King. Hams are cooked for approximately four hours with light seasoning. About 2,000-3,000 pounds of meat are cooked each week.

    The Beacon offers pork in two forms: sliced and "outside." Outside is literally the more seasoned exterior pieces of the ham which are cooked more than the inside pieces. It is chopped into bite-sized pieces, mixed with sauce and then cooked again. A little tough and chewy, the outside had a delicious, savory flavor. The sliced pork contained little fat. The pork was accented by a sauce that seems to be a native of the northwest corner of South Carolina. Developed over 40 years ago and containing vinegar, cloves, nutmeg and other spices, it has a tomato base. The sauce is so popular that Mr. White sells it by the pint to his customers. Just as popular is the barbecue slaw, a sweet concoction that goes well on burgers as well as on barbecue sandwiches. Two other barbecue specialites are the sliced beef and the hash, a mild, all-beef dish whose taste may vary slightly from batch to batch. The servings are always generous, and as one loyal fan remarked, "You'll never go away from the Beacon hungry!" The extensive menu includes almost 60 different sandwiches, fish, other seafood and chicken. Whole red hams, pork hams, turkeys, as well as all the barbecue items, may be purchased by the pound.

-109-

THE PLACE:

Just visiting the Beacon and watching the lightning efficiency with which the customers are served is an experience itself. You cannot be shy at the hectic order counter but must speak up or the order-taker will pass you by. These employees bark out the customers' requests, and someone in the huge visible kitchen area fills it almost automatically. By the time the patron has ordered and moved down the counter a few feet, it is ready. You shout your drink order and continue to move down the line until you reach the cash register. The whole process - from ordering to receiving change - usually takes only a few minutes.

A long screen separates the order counter from the seating area. Several rooms filled with booths for about 4-6 can accommodate 240 patrons. Televisions are located in various corners throughout the rooms. Large iced tea dispensers are placed next to a selection of condiments in each room. Large tinted windows overlook the huge parking area, where curb attendants lounge around, waiting to serve the drive-in customers. Usually 10-foot high mounds of bagged onions are leaning against the exterior walls, waiting to be cut and deep-fat-fried into the Beacon's famous french-fried onion rings.

* * * * * * *

SHERIDAN'S RESTAURANT

LOCATION: 827 Union St., Spartanburg 585-4712

HOURS: Mon.-Fri. 7:45 a.m. - 8 p.m.;
               Sat. 7:45 a.m. - 3 p.m.

TYPE: Regular menu and take-out

PRICES: Dinners-average; bulk rates-average

COOKING
TECHNIQUE: Electric rotisserie

THE BARCECUE:

Michael Sheridan, who has been in business since 1960, barbecues hams (to make the sliced and chopped pork) and spare ribs in an electric rotisserie cooker. Only dry seasonings are used while the meat is cooking; afterwards, a tomato-based sauce is added to the meat. Mr. Sheridan uses the commercial Barbecue King sauce. Sheridan's also serves beef hash and a full menu - mostly sandwiches.

THE PLACE:

    A typical luncheonette-type restaurant, Sheridan's can accommodate about 23 customers at a counter and at the few tables. A television, usually tuned-in to a sporting event, is the center of attention in this tiny eating establishment.

* * * * * * *

THE RANCH HOUSE BARBECUE

LOCATION: Hwy. 29 south - 5 miles south of Anderson
                 226-4456

HOURS: Mon.-Wed. 8 a.m. - 2 p.m.;
                 Thurs.-Sun. 8 a.m. - 8 p.m.

TYPE: Regular menu and take-out

PRICES: Dinners-average; bulk rates-high

COOKING
TECHNIQUE: Closed brick pit - hickory and red oak

THE BARCECUE:

    Despite several pit fires over the past 31 years, The Ranch has continued to be owned and run by Ernest Meyers and a few loyal workers. Boston butts, chicken, and pork ribs are cooked in a closed brick oven over hickory and/or red oak. About halfway through the cooking process, the meat is turned. From the Boston butts Mr. Meyers makes his sliced and minced barbecue, both of which are lean and nicely flavored with wood smoke. Complimenting the meat's flavor is a sweet tomato and spice sauce which can be purchased in pint containers. When the ribs have almost finished cooking over the fire, they are cut up and drenched in a pan of sauce. Then they are put back into the pit to finish cooking. The result is mouth-watering, large, meaty ribs that had an excellent hickory and tomato sauce flavoring. The Ranch also offers an unusual service to its customers. For $6.00 Mr. Meyers will barbecue whatever his customer brings in - hams, shoulders, turkeys or game.

THE PLACE:

    This 31-year-old restaurant is a treat for those looking for a quaint place that time doesn't appear to have touched. A large, brick fireplace occupies one side of the room. Ancient wooden booths and old plastic and metal tables and chairs seat 40 customers. An old-fashioned Coke refrigerator box holds soft drinks. A few Western touches, such as wagon wheel lighting fixtures, explain the restaurant's name.

* * * * * * *

THE CHATTER BOX

LOCATION: 1100 Pearman Dairy Rd. (Hwy. 28 bypass)
              Anderson 226-7351

HOURS: Every day 6 a.m. - 3 p.m.

TYPE: Regular menu and take-out

PRICES: Dinners-average; bulk rates-average

COOKING
TECHNIQUE: Electric

THE BARCECUE:

Owner Danny Cone gained much of his restaurant and barbecuing experience while working as a federal meat inspector for the U.S. Department of Agriculture. Using his knowledge of selecting meats, Mr. Cone started his restaurant in 1976 and is quite proud of the barbecue he serves. In an electric oven he cooks Boston butts and shoulders for 6-8 hours. Seasoning ingredients and techniques are his own, and he refuses to divulge them. The sauce he makes is a sweet, mild mustard/ketchup combination. The chopped barbecue was lean and flavorful. Barbecue plates are served with baked beans and slaw. Besides barbecue, the Chatter Box specializes in fresh vegetables and home-cooked meals.

THE PLACE:

The Chatter Box has a front porch atmosphere with its green gingham curtains, lime-green "lattice" work wall paper, and hanging plants. A comfortable dining room seats 40, and a smaller room with a counter and booths seats 30. Large windows overlook the parking lot.

* * * * * * *

LITTLE PIGS BARBECUE OF ANDERSON

LOCATION: Camp Shopping Center, Anderson   226-7388

HOURS: Mon.-Sat. 10 a.m. - 9 p.m.

TYPE: Regular menu and take out

PRICES: Dinners-average; Bulk rates-high

COOKING
TECHNIQUE: Electric-cooked - hickory-smoked

THE BARCECUE:

    Mr. and Mrs. Joe R. Dukes have owned and operated Little Pigs Barbecue since 1965, when it was still part of the Memphis-based franchise. Mr. Dukes cooks Boston butts for 8-10 hours on an electric Bar-B-Q King cooker, smoking the meat with hickory chips throughout the process. After it is cooked and chopped, the meat is sauced. Various kinds of sandwiches are also on the menu.

THE PLACE:

    Located at one end of a small shopping center, Little Pigs Barbecue has a glass front that looks out into the parking lot. Booths and tables-for-four seat about 50 people. Drinks may be purchased from two large Pepsi machines near the front. Customers order at a walk-up counter near the rear.

* * * * * * *

RICK'S BAR-B-Q

LOCATION: On the McCormick Hwy. (Hwy. 10), 4 miles
                 from Greenwood   223-8395

HOURS: Fri.-Sat. 5 p.m. - 8:30 a.m.

TYPE: Buffet, take-out and catering

PRICES: Buffet-average; bulk rates-average

COOKING
TECHNIQUE: Electric cooker - hickory-smoked

THE BARCECUE:

    For the first 10-11 years after opening in 1961, owner John T. Rickenbaker hickory-smoked his barbecue on an open pit. Now, mostly for convenience, Rickenbaker has moved to the electric pit with attached hickory smoker. He uses only whole hams (about 20 per cooking), cooked 8 hours and smoked during the last 45 minutes, to make his chopped barbecue. The sauce, a mustard/ketchup mixture cooked with a broth of ham bones and skins, is mixed with the meat after it has been chopped. The finished product, lean chips of pork, has a spicy, peppery taste, and some of the larger chunks have a crunchy outer edge. Simmering in black kettles, Rick's hash is made with half beef and half pork. Also on the all-you-can-eat buffet are fried chicken, livers and gizzards, slaw, sweet potatoes and loaf bread. Rick's biggest business is done on the 4th of July, when he serves about nine tons of barbecue.

THE PLACE:

     Amidst trees and blooming countryside sits Ricks' Bar-B-Q, a large open building with a cement floor and no frills. One hundred and thirty-eight customers can be accommodated at the long folding tables. Take-out orders are prepared and sold at a counter at the back of the building.

* * * * * * *

LITTLE PIGS OF GREENWOOD

LOCATION: 414 Montague Ave. Extension, Greenwood
                229-1314

HOURS: Mon.-Sat. 10:30 a.m. - 8:30 p.m.

TYPE: Regular menu, take-out and catering

PRICES: Dinners-average; bulk rates-average

COOKING
TECHNIQUE: Electric cooker - hickory-smoked

THE BARBECUE:

     In 1964 when Little Pigs opened, it was still affiliated with Little Pigs Barbecue of America, and the barbecue was still cooked on an open pit with wood. Seven years ago, though, according to owner Mary Scott, the restaurant switched to cooking electrically. To make her chopped barbecue Mrs. Scott uses hams, cooked about 8 hours and smoked with hickory chips. The sauce, a homemade concoction that tastes more of ketchup than anything else, tastes very similar to the sauces served at the other Little Pigs Barbecues across the state. The chopped, lean meat has no smoked flavor. Barbecue plates are served with cole slaw and barbecued beans. A full menu, including homemade chicken salad, is offered.

THE PLACE:

Little Pigs of Greenwood is a small restaurant containing tables and chairs for about 56. The menu is located on the wall above the counter where the customer places his order. Drinks may be purchased from a Coke machine near the counter.

* * * * * * *

OLD HICKORY RESTAURANT

LOCATION: 15 miles west of Spartanburg - 299 Spartanburg Hwy. (Hwy. 29), Lyman 439-9011

HOURS: Mon.-Sat. 6:30 a.m. - 8 p.m.

TYPE: Regular menu and take-out

PRICES: Dinners-low; bulk rates-average

COOKING
TECHNIQUE: Electric

THE BARBECUE:

In 1972 a tornado destroyed the building that stood in the location of the Old Hickory Restaurant. Mr. Leo George bought the remains and built a new restaurant, which he opened in July 1974. George did not lack barbecue experience before opening his business. For eleven years he learned the secrets of barbecuing by working at the Beacon, a long-time institution in Spartanburg. To make his sliced barbecue, the proprietor cooks hams for 5-7 hours on an electric pit. He slices the pork into medium-sized pieces and offers the customer a choice of two sauces. One is a thin, spicy homemade mixture which he sells by the pint. The other is Bennett's Chili Sauce, a sweet, tomatoey mixture with an abundance of peppers and relish. To make a deluxe sandwich, Mr. George tops the pork with a mixture of slaw and his sauce and then adds a heap of the chili sauce. The slices of pork tasted like roast pork with very little seasoning. The barbecued beef was thinly sliced and a little dry, but it was lean and more flavorful than the pork. Also on the menu, along with hot dogs, hamburgers, steak, seafood and chicken, is barbecue hash, made with 100% beef and simmered slowly all night. The hash had a spicy, slightly oniony flavor.

THE PLACE:

Located in a new-looking brick building adjoining a few commercial shops, the Hickory House restaurant has two dining rooms separated by a work area and counter. Seating on stools at the counter and in molded plastic chairs at formica-topped tables for four totals 110. The rooms are decorated in bright spring colors, with white lattice work painted on the lime green walls and green curtains on the windows. Hanging baskets and plants adorn the dining area.

* * * * * * *

PIG-N-CHICK

LOCATION:	401 Miller Rd. (corner of Mill Rd. and Miller Rd.), Mauldin 288-7042
HOURS:	Mon.-Sat. 11 a.m. - 9:30 p.m.
TYPE:	Regular menu (cafeteria style), take-out and catering
PRICES:	Dinners-average; bulk rates-average
COOKING TECHNIQUE:	Electric cooker (rotisserie) - hickory-smoked

THE BARBECUE:

The former "Happy Jack's Bar-B-Q" has changed names and locations. The owner is still Ed Seibold, who has been in the restaurant business several years. According to manager Ron Sauder, hams and shoulders are cooked on an electric rotisserie and smoked with hickory chips. The finely chopped barbecued pork was lean and had a slight hickory flavor. The mild sauce, a 20-year-old recipe, is an uncooked tomato-based mixture. The move to the new location has brought about several changes. Seibold has introduced a new sauce -- a mustard-based one -- to compete with his old standby. Besides chopped pork, ribs and chicken are barbecued. The meaty ribs were lightly seasoned and accompanied by a pleasant tomato sauce. Chicken comes in a variety of forms at Pig-N-Chick. In addition to being barbecued, it is chopped and made into salad for sandwiches. A new menu item is a 3 ounce chicken breast, marinated in rich barbecue sauce and then deep-fat-fried. Brunswick stew, a chicken/beef combination, is made from an old Georgia recipe. Sandwiches and barbecued beans are still being served, and a salad bar has been added.

THE PLACE:

Around the interior perimeter of the restaurant are roomy orange booths, and along with tables and chairs, the dining room can seat 98 customers. Located on one wall is a cafeteria set-up. Customer walk through the line and select their food. Meat is kept warm in three hot steamers until it is served. A large glass deli case, displaying delectable meats, is a focal point in the room. Pig-N-Chick soon hopes to add drive-up window service.

* * * * * * *

LITTLE PIGS BARBECUE

LOCATION: 522 Mills Ave., Greenville   235-7211

HOURS: Mon.-Sat. 9:30 a.m. - 8 p.m.

TYPE: Regular menu and take-out

PRICES: Dinners-low; bulk rates-high

COOKING
TECHNIQUE: Gas and lava rock

THE BARBECUE:

* * * * * * *

Eighteen years ago when Wilbur E. and Douglas L. Rogers opened Little Pigs, it was still part of the Memphis-based Little Pigs of America franchise. Now Wilbur and Douglas own their restaurant outright. For fifteen hours pork shoulders are cooked over gas and lava rock, a kind of briquet that gives the meat a special flavor when the dripping grease produces smoke. Mr. Rogers places the cooked shoulders under a gas flame behind the counter until ready to be served. As needed, he cuts off a slab of meat, chops it in view of the customer and prepares the order. No sauce is applied until the sandwiches or plates are fixed. The proprietors still use the original Little Pigs sauce recipes. One sauce is a mildly seasoned, tomatoey mixture; the other's hotness makes it almost overpowering. Both may be purchased by the pint. The hotter sauce has a large dose of Texas Pete-like flavoring. The chopped barbecue was crusty and tasty, made even better with only a slight sprinkling of the hot sauce. Mr. Rogers recommended the homemade baked beans, one of their most popular menu items, to accompany the barbecue. Burgers and a few sandwiches are available.

THE PLACE:

This tiny restaurant contains a walk-up order counter with the menu posted on the wall. Small wooden tables and chairs seat about 34.

* * * * * * *

LITTLE PIGS BARBECUE

LOCATION: Lake Forest Shopping Center (off Hwy. 291 By-Pass), Greenville 244-6030

HOURS: Mon.-Sat. 9:30 a.m. - 8:30 p.m.

TYPE: Regular menu and take-out

PRICES: Dinners-low; bulk rates-high

COOKING TECHNIQUE: Gas

THE BARBECUE:

Although under different ownership, the Little Pigs Barbecue in this location serves barbecue that is almost identical to that served at Little Pigs Barbeque on Mills Ave.

THE PLACE:

The building restaurant set-up is quite similar to the other Greenville Little Pigs.

INDEX

Bar-B-Q Hut Restaurant	Sumter	104
Bar-B-Query-J.D. Hite & Son, The	West Columbia	31
Barbeque Diner	North Augusta	81
Beacon Drive-In	Spartanburg	109
Bessinger's Bar-B-Q	Charleston	40
Bessinger's Barbeque House (2)	Charleston	39
Big D's Bar-B-Q I	Hemingway, near	69
Big D's Bar-B-Q I	Johsonville, near	69
Big D's Bar-B-Q II	Surfside Beach	70
Black's Bar-B-Q	Barnwell	84
Bo-Corley's Bar-B-Q	Barnwell	85
Bob's Bar-B-Q	Florence	64
Boney's Bar-B-Que	Ridgeway	96
Broome's Restaurant	Kershaw	97
Brown Derby Bar-B-Q	Orangeburg	51
Buddy's Hickory Cooked Bar-B-Q	Chester	93
Cain's Bar-B-Q	Florence	62
Carolina Bar-B-Q	New Ellenton	75
Chatter Box, The	Anderson	112
Chavous Pit Cooked Bar-B-Q	Beech Island	76
Country Cousin Bar-B-Que	Scranton	59
Country Pit Bar-B-Que	North Augusta	82
Cowan's Ranch Bar-B-Que	Columbia	24
Crosby's Bar-B-Q	New Ellenton	74
D & H Bar-B-Q	Manning	105
Daniel's and Ray's Barbecue	Nichols	65
David Brown's House Pit Bar-B-Q	Winnsboro	89
Drozes Bar-B-Q	Summerville	48
Duke's Bar-B-Q	Orangeburg	50
Duke's BBQ	Orangeburg	49
Duke's BBQ	St. George	48
Dukes BBQ	Fairfax	88
Earl Duke's Bar-B-Q	Cameron	52
Ed Neeley's Bar-B-Q	Denmark	87
Edmunds Bar-B-Que	Aiken	80
Edmunds Bar-B-Que	North Augusta	79
Fat Willy's Hawg House	Rock Hill	93
Fat Willy's Hawg House	Fort Mill	93
Fennell's Bar-B-Q	Hampton	47
Fred Gaskins' Grocery	Lake City	60
Freeman's BBQ	Beech Island	78
Fulmer's Bar-B-Q	Aiken	74
Hammy's Bar-B-Q House	Elgin	102
Hilltop Restaurant	Great Falls	95
Hites Restaurant	Lexington	19
Keith's Barbecue	Beaufort	45
Keith's Barbecue	North Charleston	43
Keith's Red Barn	Walterboro	42
Laird's Bar-B-Q	North	53
Lee's Bar-B-Q	North Augusta	83
Lester's Pit Bar-B-Q	Estill, near	46
Lester's Pit Bar-B-Q	Hampton, near	46
Little Betsy's Bar-B-Q Rest.	McBee	98
Little Pigs Bar-B-Que	Columbia	18
Little Pigs Barbecue	Greenville	117

Name	Location	Page
Little Pigs Barbecue	Greenville	118
Little Pigs Barbeque of Anderson	Anderson	113
Little Pigs of Greenwood	Greenwood	114
Maurice's Piggy Park	West Columbia	21
Mett's Bar-B-Q	Bamberg	86
Midland Kitchen	Columbia	25
Midway BBQ	Union	92
Moree's Bar-B-Q	Andrews	57
Muldrow's Bar-B-Que	Columbia	29
Oak Grove Bar-B-Q House	West Columbia	23
Okra Patch	Irmo	32
Old Hickory Restaurant	Spartanburg	115
Owen's Bar-B-Q	Lake City	61
Pig-N-Chick	Mauldin	116
Piggy Park	Mt. Pleasant	41
Pinetucket Bar-B-Q Barn	Aynor	66
Pit, The	Columbia	28
Porky's Bar-B-Q	Columbia	30
Que Pit, The	Newberry	71
Radd Dew's Bar-B-Q	Conway	67
Ranch House Barbecue, The	Anderson	111
Rast's Restaurant	Johns Island	44
Ray Lever's Bar-B-Q Hut	Blythewood	35
Red Barn Bar-B-Q, The	Windy Hill Beach	68
Revel's Barbecue Center	Bennettsville	100
Reynold's Bar-B-Q	Camden	101
Rick's Bar-B-Q	Greenwood	113
Rogers Bar-B-Que	Hardeeville	55
Sam's Bar-B-Q	Columbia	33
Sawgrass Jim's Bar-B-Q House	Spartanburg	107
Shady Rest Park, The	Columbia	26
Shealy Bar-B-Q Buffet Style	Leesville	17
Sheridan's Restaurant	Spartanburg	110
Shiloh BBQ	Chesterfield	99
Sike's Bar-B-Q	Eastover	34
Smith's Bar-B-Que	Columbia	27
Smokey Porkers Bar-B-Q	Beech Island	77
Stockman's Bar-B-Q Place	Prosperity	73
Sweatman's Bar-B-Que	Eutawville, near	37
Sweatman's Bar-B-Que	Holly Hill, near	37
Tisdale's Bar-B-Q	Kingstree, near	58
Ward's Bar-B-Q	Columbia	36
Ward's Bar-B-Q	Columbia (1)	103
Ward's Bar-B-Q	Sumter (4)	103
Westwood Bar-B-Q	Hartsville	90
Willard's BBQ and Hash House	Gaffney	94
Wise's Bar-B-Q	Newberry	72
Woody's Barbecue	Florence	63

TO: THE SANDLAPPER STORE, INC.
     P.O. Box 841
     Lexington, South Carolina 29072

Please send me _____ copies of Hog Heaven at $3.95* per copy plus 75¢ per copy (for postage and handling). Orders for 5 or more books postpaid. S.C. residents add 4% sales tax to the cost of the books.

Name _____

Street _____

State & Zip _____

*price subject to change

TO: THE SANDLAPPER STORE, INC.
     P.O. Box 841
     Lexington, South Carolina 29072

Please send me _____ copies of Hog Heaven at $3.95* per copy plus 75¢ per copy (for postage and handling). Orders for 5 or more books postpaid. S.C. residents add 4% sales tax to the cost of the books.

Name _____

Street _____

State & Zip _____

*price subject to change

TO: THE SANDLAPPER STORE, INC.
     P.O. Box 841
     Lexington, South Carolina 29072

Please send me _____ copies of Hog Heaven at $3.95* per copy plus 75¢ per copy (for postage and handling). Orders for 5 or more books postpaid. S.C. residents add 4% sales tax to the cost of the books.

Name _____

Street _____

State & Zip _____

*price subject to change